Blackjack Gold

**A New Approach
To
Winning
At
"21"**

Lancelot Humble Ph.D.

International Gaming Incorporated
Toronto, 1976

This book is dedicated to all those who have attempted the
game of casino blackjack and wished they could have played
better. With this book they can realize their wishes.

PUBLISHED BY

International Gaming Incorporated

25 Johnson Avenue

Thornhill, Ontario, Canada L3T 2N8

First printing - October, 1976

Library of Congress Catalog Number
ISBN Number   0-920228-00-3

WHAT THIS BOOK WILL DO FOR YOU

This is the first book that teaches you how to win money in a casino. Winning strategies, techniques, and moves are described that will enable you to win even under adverse conditions. This book is not theoretical. It deals with the harsh realities of casino gambling. The book presents a pragmatic approach to WINNING at the game, not just playing it. The approach is based on over 30 trips to Las Vegas and other casinos and on hundreds of hours of successful casino gaming experience. This is the simplest and most practical book ever written on blackjack.

YOU WILL LEARN:

- How to play a simple winning strategy against any number of decks.
- How to spot a cheating dealer.
- How to slow down a fast dealer.
- Five wagering methods to suit all conditions.
- When to bet a lot, when to bet the minimum, when to quit.
- How to identify safe and unsafe casinos.
- How to avoid getting barred.
- How to play like a professional.

FORWARD

by Edward O. Thorp

Blackjack Gold is an excellent book for the beginning blackjack
player. It presents the simple but powerful HI-OPT point count
and the correct fixed BASIC STRATEGY for one, two, and four
decks. The strategy for varying the play of the hand with the
count is not included. There are many practical tips and ob-
servations which can be of great value to both beginning players
and experts.

EDWARD O. THORP
October 19, 1976

AKNOWLEDGEMENTS

I wish to thank all the scholars who have participated in the
evolution of the game over the years. In particular, I wish
to thank Edward O. Thorp and Julian H. Braun for their original
work and for their important recent contributions.

INTRODUCTION

by Julian H. Braun

This is a fascinating, informative, and surprising book.
During the past 14 years as a direct consequence of the work
of Dr. Edward O. Thorp, myself, and others, numerous methods of winning
at blackjack by means of count systems have developed. For the serious
player who will take the trouble to properly learn and use one of the
better systems the player can and should win over a period of time.
Yet, many such players have failed to come anywhere near the mathematically proven reasonable expectations. There is more to playing
the game than just knowing what is the mathematically correct play --
much more. Dr. Humble, whose major profession is psychology and whose
avocation is the scientific exploitation of gambling has woven both
factors into a fascinating account of just how to really succeed at
casino blackjack. This account includes a surprisingly thorough discussion of the current situation of cheating in the casinos with recommendations on how to succeed in spite of it. For legal reasons the
names of specific casinos where certain incidents took place are re-
placed by humorous pseudonyms.

There is much to learn in this book for both the novice and the
experienced player. As a result of this book the reader is not
guaranteed that he will win, but his chances of doing so will surely
improve markedly in proportion to the degree that he masters and
applies the information.

JULIAN H. BRAUN
CHICAGO, ILLINOIS
October 10, 1976

PREFACE

Purpose

Someone once said that there are three kinds of people in this world: those that make things happen, those that watch things happen, and those that wonder what happened. The purpose of this book is to keep you from falling into the last category when you attempt blackjack.

Apology to the Residents of Las Vegas

The attacks in this book are not aimed at you. I like you. You have been kind to me. The attacks are aimed at the people associated with certain casinos. I do not like them. They have been cruel to me. Those hypocrites cheated me and stole my hard earned money. On the whole, Las Vegas is like other tourist cities, except the trap is bigger and the bait more attractive.

Statement to Legal Agents

This book is to be regarded as a novel, the contents as pure fiction. The author and publisher cannot assume responsibility for any gambling losses incurred by readers or casinos as a result of this book. However, the author will accept a percentage of all winnings resulting from this book.

A Word to the Reader

There is much truth in "fiction".

A Challenge to the Skeptics

You say you don't believe that blackjack is a game of skill? I invite you to be the dealer. Any of my students will be glad to demonstrate how easy it is to win. We have an open challenge to play any person or casino for any amount up to $50,000.

CONTENTS

WHAT THIS BOOK WILL DO FOR YOU

FORWARD by Edward O. Thorp

INTRODUCTION by Julian H. Braun

PREFACE

       Purpose. Apology To The Residents Of Las Vegas. Statement To
Legal Agents. A Word To The Reader. A Challenge To The
Skeptics.

       Myth #1 - You Need Luck In Order To Win At Casino Blackjack.
Myth #2 - You Have To Be A Mathematical Genius In Order To Learn
How To Win At Blackjack. Myth #3 - You Have To Have A Photographic
Memory In Order To Learn How To Win At Blackjack. Myth #4 - Dealers
Deal Too Fast For Players To Be Able To Keep Track Of Cards And Win.
Myth #5 - It Is Impossible To Win Playing Against Four Decks Because
There Are 208 Cards To Keep Track Of. Myth #6 - You Need A Bankroll
of Thousands Of Dollars In Order To Win Appreciable Amounts Of
Money At Blackjack. Myth #7 - There Is No Cheating In Large Las
Vegas Casinos. Myth #8 - They Only Cheat High Rollers. Myth #9 -
Bad Players Have An Adverse Effect On A Good Player's Game. Myth
#10 - The Player At Third Base Can Have A Greater Effect On Whether
The Dealer Busts Or Not Than Any Other Players At The Table. Myth
#11 - Casinos Use Shills In Order To Cheat Players. Culture Shock.

       Basic Strategy For One Deck. Basic Strategy For Four Or More Decks.
Exceptional Situations. Basic Strategy For Two Decks. How To
Learn The Basic Strategy. Practice Table.

       HI-OPT Count. Practice Card Combinations. Insurance.

       Step 1. Step 2. Step 3. Step 4.

1. A Complete Knowledge Of The Game. 2. The Keeping Of Records.
3. Self-Knowledge. 4. Independence Of Thought And Confidence.
5. Mental Readiness Or Total Concentration. 6. Physical Readiness.
7. A Basic Knowledge Of Probability Theory. 8. Self-Control.
9. A Game Plan.

Gambling As An Altered State of Consciousness.

The Burn Card And The Bottom Card. Cutting The Deck. Mixing Your
Chips. The Team Approach To The Shoe Game. Disguises. Talk To
The Pit Boss Before Playing. The Advantages Of Being Female. Gambling
Is Good For You. Play Alone. Adopt A Spy Mentality. Your Bet Range.
Hide Your Winnings. Decks With A Border. Playing Two Or More Hands.
Pick Your Dealer Carefully. Controls Over Emotions. Casinos With
Favourable Rules. Get Change Immediately For Tipping. The Blackjack
Dealer. Table DK-RS: Decks And Rules Variations In Las Vegas As Of
September, 1976. How Much Should I Bet For The Dealer? The Cut-Off
Dealer. Quitting For The Day. Don't Turn Your Head. The Face-Up
Game. Going To The Washroom. Keeping Separate Track Of Aces. The
Trailer. Fear Of Getting Barred. Tough-Looking Dealers. Blackjack
Games In Canada. One Good Sign Of A Cheating Dealer. The Author's
Position On Dealer Cheating. The Cheating Can Be Eliminated. Memory
Aids. "Heat". "Help". Gambling Conference.

APPENDIX

The HI-OPT. The HI-OPT II. The International Blackjack Club.
Order Coupons For Blackjack Gold.

1   THE GAME

Blackjack is a unique casino game. Blackjack is unique because it is the only casino game in which the player can win money by using his or her skill. In blackjack the player can learn how to get a permanent advantage on the house. This is not possible in any other casino game. There are a number of computer devised winning strategies for casino blackjack. One simple and effective strategy will be presented for you in this book. It is very important to realize that blackjack is the only casino game in which the player can actually have an advantage on the casino. All the other games -- craps, roulette, baccarat, keno, and the slot machines -- are rigged in such a way as to give the casino a permanent advantage. There is no way that anyone can win at these games. There is one exception, and that is if someone plays for a very short time and gets lucky. By getting lucky I mean the fluctuations of the dice or the wheels in the slot machine or the ball in roulette temporarily go in his direction. He can win money providing he quits and never plays again. If a person should come back and try to win more money, as 99 out of every 100 gamblers try to do, the mathematical percentages will simply grind the person down. He will lose all his money. And the longer he gambles the more money he will lose. This is a mathematical reality that has been demonstrated not just with computers and not just by mathematicians but in casinos by players playing thousands of hours and testing the different games with thousands of different systems. So let's clear that up right now. You should realize that there is no sense even attempting to play any of the other games because they are all losing propositions in the long run. No system has ever beaten those games. And no system ever will beat those other games as they are now played. If you want to be a winner in casino gambling you must choose blackjack as your game.

2   THE ROAD TO WINNING

Here is a step by step summary of what you need in order to win money in a casino. This summary is placed at the beginning of the book to help you focus your reading.

Learn the HI-OPT count by practising at home.
Learn the basic strategy by practising at home.
Combine the count and the basic strategy and play
    blackjack at home.
Use the count to vary your wagers.
Use the basic strategy to play your hands correctly.
    Never deviate from the basic strategy.
Keep records of your wins and losses at home.
Continue playing at home until you have won at least
    500 units. Keep playing if you are still not
    convinced that you have a winning system.
Accumulate an adequate bankroll.
Locate a casino that is in the top ten
    in terms of safety according to Table P.
Locate a table with a young female dealer.
Begin to play and keep playing against this dealer
    until you are showing a profit.
Keep playing as long as you are winning.
Quit as soon as you begin to lose or as soon as
    another dealer comes to your table.
Record the events of the playing session on your
    Record Sheet.
After quitting, leave the casino quickly.
Find someone to cash your chips for you or come
    back at another time and cash them yourself.
Repeat the whole process in another safe casino.

That is the beginning of the road to winning.

3 THE ROAD TO LOSING

Philosophers sometimes use the technique of <u>opposites</u> in order to make a point. The purpose of this book is to show you how to win. On this page I do the opposite. I show you how to lose. The purpose of this exercise is to alert you to potentially losing situations.

Read this book quickly.

Assume you know the count and the basic strategy well enough to win.

Ignore the chapters on cheating dealers since you "know" they don't cheat in Las Vegas.

Rush to Las Vegas with any kind of a bankroll.

Find a casino that is in the worst ten in terms of safety according to Table P.

Sit down at a twenty-five dollar minimum table.

Make sure the dealer is a male over 30 years of age.

Buy chips with your entire bankroll.

Try to play to the best of your ability even though you are tired because of the long flight and because you didn't sleep well last night.

Be prepared to leave Las Vegas in 20 minutes.

You have just lost all your money.

I am deadly serious about the road to losing. If you doubt it, try it. The road to losing is a super expressway. The road to winning is a turtle path going up a steep mountain.

4   MYTHS IN BLACKJACK

There are several myths about blackjack which should be dispelled first. These myths have clouded the thinking of many potential blackjack champions. Each myth will be shattered in this volume.   In this way the air will be cleared for the person interested in learning how to play winning blackjack. Here is a list of the myths. They will be dealt with in detail below.

Myth #1 - Blackjack is a game of luck.
Myth #2 - You have to be a mathematical genius in order to learn how to win at blackjack.
Myth #3 - You have to have a photographic memory to learn how to win at blackjack.
Myth #4 - The dealers deal too fast for a player to be able to keep track of the cards and win.
Myth #5 - It is very difficult if not impossible to win playing against four decks being dealt out of a shoe.
Myth #6 - You need a bankroll of thousands of dollars in order to win good money at blackjack.
Myth #7 - There is no cheating in large Las Vegas casinos.
Myth #8 - Dealers only cheat players who bet a lot of money.
Myth #9 - Bad players have an adverse effect on the chances of a good player playing at the same table.
Myth #10- The player sitting at third base can have a greater effect on whether the dealer busts or makes his hand than any of the other players.
Myth #11- Casinos use shills dressed as other players who work with the dealer to draw certain cards away from the player.

The eleven myths will now be explored. All the myths should be completely shattered for you by the time you finish reading this book.

Myth #1 - <u>You need luck in order to win at casino blackjack</u>.

This is a completely false belief. Casino blackjack is the only casino game in which the player can actually get a permanent, long-term, mathematical advantage on the house, using skill. Luck has nothing whatsoever to do with a player winning or losing money at casino blackjack in the long run once the player has learned the basic strategy and a simple method of keeping track of cards. True, in the short-run, which could be over a period of a few playing sessions, the player may win a lot more than his advantage would dictate or he may lose a lot more than his advantage would dictate. However, in the long-run the player who knows how to play a winning game will realize exactly the percentage of profit that is indicated by the mathematical advantage of the strategy which he is employing. The skeptical reader can prove this for himself by learning a certain strategy and by playing a few thousand hands of blackjack at home, keeping track of the results of each hand. Or if he has a computer at his disposal, he can ask the computer to do the playing. Either way the player will show a profit after playing a few thousand hands.

Myth #2 - <u>You have to be a mathematical genius in order to learn how to win at blackjack</u>.

This is a myth which began after a mathematics professor, Edward Thorp, published his best-seller <u>Beat the Dealer</u> in 1962. Thorp did have a very complicated strategy in his book which he called the ten count. The press and other media focused on his being a professor and came to the erroneous conclusion that only a person with a professor's intelligence could win at blackjack. The fact is that if the reporters had read Thorp's book they would have found a very simple point-count(where one kept track of the small cards by calling them plus 1 each and the tens and aces by calling them minus one each as they were dealt out of the deck.)

This simple point count along with the basic strategy, which
simply consisted of three charts found in the middle of his book,
is all that one needs to learn in order to be a winning player.
I taught a ten-year-old girl and a twelve-year-old boy, in one
weekend, while we were on a holiday, to play a winning game using
the above method.

Myth #3 - You have to have a photographic memory in order to learn
how to win at blackjack. This myth is totally false. As was
pointed out in Myth #2, all you need is a simple point count with
which to keep track of cards along with the basic strategy in order
to win. Even Lawrence Revere, who markets many count strategies,
admits this simple fact. It has been my experience, in teaching
people how to play blackjack privately, that most people have much
more difficulty learning the basic strategy chart than they do
keeping track of the cards. Thus, I conclude that the most difficult part about learning how to win at blackjack is learning the
basic strategy. And this can be learned in only a few hours. No
photographic memory or anything approaching such a memory is needed.
All that is needed is a few hours of practice and memory work.

Myth #4 - Dealers deal too fast for players to be able to keep
track of cards and win. While it is true that a lot of dealers deal
extremely fast it is not true that fast dealing makes it impossible
for you to keep track of cards. Why? Simply because no dealer can
deal past you until you give him the signal that you are finished.
That is, how can a dealer deal fast when he doesn't know whether
you want to hit or not, or whether you want to double your bet or
not, or whether you want to split your pairs or not? It is true
that some dealers try to get you in their rhythm of playing. They
will begin dealing slowly and then very, very gradually speed up
their dealing, getting you to play faster and faster. They do this
so expertly and so gradually that you don't realize until later that

you are being rushed. By this time you allow yourself to be rushed because you don't want to feel that you cannot keep up. What is happening here is that the dealer is intimidating you. And you, (because of your inflated ego) don't want to admit that you are being intimidated. You stubbornly refuse to take your time and slow the dealer down. You must, right from the beginning, as soon as you sit down to play, signal the dealer clearly on every hand so that he is always expecting and waiting for your signal. In this way he can never deal too fast for you to keep track of the cards.

Myth #5 - It is impossible to win playing against four decks because there are 208 cards to keep track of.

It is true that four decks all mixed in together do seem formidable. However, it only takes a little more mental effort to keep track of 208 cards than it does with 52 cards. It simply takes longer and is more fatiguing mentally because the dealer doesn't shuffle up as often. In the single deck, because the dealer shuffles up so often, your mind gets a chance to rest while he is shuffling. It is no more difficult mentally keeping track of the individual cards when you are using a simple plus-minus point count. There are no extra different kinds of cards to keep track of in a four deck game - all cards are either plus one or minus one, or plus two or minus two, for example. All you have to do is keep track of them four times the amount of time at one span compared to the single deck game. If you find that you do have trouble keeping your concentration for that long I advise that you buy four decks, mix them together, and practise keeping track of the cards at home. Your four deck card counting will quickly become habitual with a little mental strain.

Myth #6 - You need a bankroll of thousands of dollars in order to win appreciable amounts of money at blackjack.

All you need is a bankroll of $100. With such a small bankroll you can win thousands of dollars playing blackjack. Admittedly, it will take you much longer if you start with a small

bankroll because you will only be able to make small bets,
$1 and $2 bets, and you will win only small amounts of money at
first. But you will win at the same rate as anybody betting $100
chips. Thus, the more hours that you play, the more money you
will have accumulated. Then, of course, once you double your
bankroll to $200 you can bet twice as much on each bet and so on.
After the first few dozen hours of play you will be making bigger
and bigger bets and will be well on your way to winning thousands
of dollars if you want to stay with the game. No large bankroll
is needed at first. What is of critical importance is that you
learn to play accurately without making mistakes and that you
learn how to stay out of cheating casinos and away from cheating
dealers. The purpose of this book is to help you do this.

Myth #7 - There is no cheating in large Las Vegas casinos.
        It has been my experience that the larger the casino the
more expert the cheating dealers are. I have been cheated out of
thousands and thousands of dollars by dealers in the largest casinos in the world.

Myth #8 - They only cheat high rollers.
        A cheating dealer will cheat anybody he wants to, whether
the person is making $1 bets, $5 bets, $25 bets, $100 bets or $500
bets. They do not discriminate.

Myth #9 - Bad players have an adverse effect on a good player's game.
        It has been proven mathematically that a bad player or bad
players at the table help the good player as often as they hinder
him in actual casino playing. Professor Peter Griffin, a mathe-
matician, has also proven this using a computer. Never blame another
player for your losses. Praise him when he helps your hand.

Myth #10 - The player at third base can have a greater effect on
whether the dealer busts or not than any other player at the table.
        This only appears to be true because he is the last player
to draw and all the other players' attention is focused upon him.

It can easily be seen that this is a myth because any player
at the table who draws or doubles, or splits, or doesn't draw
for that matter, has an effect on the other cards that the other
players will get. Therefore, it doesn't matter who goes last.
What matters, in terms of having an effect on the dealer's hand,
is how many and what kinds of cards are drawn by all the players
together.

Myth #11 - Casinos use shills in order to cheat players.
        In all my years of playing I have never seen a shill being
used in order to cheat me. True, some casinos do use shills in
order to attract other players to the table. These shills never
double down or split. But, as has been pointed out in Myth #9,
how other players at the table play their hands has absolutely no
long-term effect on a good players advantage or disadvantage.

Culture Shock
        It is very difficult to disprove a myth. I do not expect
you to change all of your false beliefs as a result of the information presented above. The information comes from my experiences
as a player. I've been there. If you haven't had the playing experience yet I hope that my experiences prove instructive to you.
You should at least be more alert as to what to expect from a
casino. I hope you don't suffer CULTURE SHOCK when you discover the
truth about the myths. (CULTURE SHOCK occurs when you learn that
everything you were ever taught to believe is false. Remember
Nixon and Agnew?)

5   THE BASIC STRATEGY

The basic strategy tells the player how to play every hand
in the game accurately. The basic strategy tells the player what
to do after he gets his original two cards from the dealer. The
strategy tells the player when his hand should be hit (ask for
additional cards), when he should stand pat, when he should
double down (double his bet on his original two cards) and whether
he should split a pair should he be dealt a pair.

Memorizing the basic strategy is a critical first step
towards learning to win at casino blackjack. The strategy was
scientifically calculated to give the player the best percentage
play for every hand dealt. Mr. Julian Braun of the IBM Corporation
is largely responsible for the basic strategy. He asked the computers to play millions of hands in order to determine the optimum play
of each hand. If one uses the basic strategy in single deck games
he will have an exactly even chance with the house. In a four
deck game the casino will have only a half of one per cent advantage in the long run. In a later step in learning to win, with
the help of a card count, the player will learn how to obtain a
permanent long term advantage on the house. Another reason the
basic strategy is so important is that the player will be using it
to play 75% of all the hands he will ever get, even though he may
be using a more sophisticated strategy later on.

The easiest form in which to learn the basic strategy is
from a chart.

Chart B-1 contains the basic strategy for single deck play.

Chart B-4 contains the basic strategy for four or more decks.
The basic strategy for two decks is the same as the strategy for
four or more decks, except for the differences indicated at the
bottom of Chart B-4.

Charts B-1 and B-4 assume that doubling down is not allowed
after pair splitting. This is the rule in most casinos. Slight
variations in the basic strategies are given at the bottom of the
charts for the case where doubling down after pair splitting is
allowed.

CHART B-1   BASIC STRATEGY FOR ONE DECK

YOUR HAND	DEALER'S UP CARD									
	2	3	4	5	6	7	8	9	10	ACE
8	H	H	H	D	D	H	H	H	H	H
9	D	D	D	D	D	H	H	H	H	H
10	D	D	D	D	D	D	D	D	H	H
11	D	D	D	D	D	D	D	D	D	D
12	H	H	S	S	S	H	H	H	H	H
13	S	S	S	S	S	H	H	H	H	H
14	S	S	S	S	S	H	H	H	H	H
15	S	S	S	S	S	H	H	H	H	H
16	S	S	S	S	S	H	H	H	H	H
17	S	S	S	S	S	S	S	S	S	S
A2	H	H	D	D	D	H	H	H	H	H
A3	H	H	D	D	D	H	H	H	H	H
A4	H	H	D	D	D	H	H	H	H	H
A5	H	H	D	D	D	H	H	H	H	H
A6	D	D	D	D	D	H	H	H	H	H
A7	S	D	D	D	D	S	S	H	H	S
A8	S	S	S	S	D	S	S	S	S	S
A9	S	S	S	S	S	S	S	S	S	S
AA	SP	SP	SP	SP	SP	SP	SP	SP	SP	SP
22	H	SP	SP	SP	SP	SP	H	H	H	H
33	H	H	SP	SP	SP	SP	H	H	H	H
66	SP	SP	SP	SP	SP	H	H	H	H	H
77	SP	SP	SP	SP	SP	SP	H	H	S	H
88	SP	SP	SP	SP	SP	SP	SP	SP	SP	SP
99	SP	SP	SP	SP	SP	S	SP	SP	S	S
1010	S	S	S	S	S	S	S	S	S	S

H - HIT   S- STAND   D- DOUBLE   SP - SPLIT
Exceptional situations for Table B-1 are given on the next page.

CHART B - 1   EXCEPTIONAL SITUATIONS

If your two card total is 7 or less, always HIT. If your two
cards are 7,7 (14) and the dealer's up card is a 10-value card,
STAND instead of hitting as the chart advises. If you have
4,4, do not split, but   consider 4,4 as 8 and follow the chart.
If you have 5,5, do not split, but   consider 5,5 as 10 and
follow the chart.

If the casino allows doubling down after pair splitting the
following changes in basic strategy apply:

    Split 2,2 vs. a dealer's 2, instead of hitting.
    Split 4,4 vs. a dealer's 4,5, or 6.
    Split 7,7 vs. a dealer's 8.

If the casino allows SURRENDER (the option to throw in your
original two-card hand and give up half of your bet) then you
would SURRENDER a 15 or a 16 against a dealer's 10-value card or
Ace, except do not surrender   8, 7 or 8, 8 and surrender a 10, 6
only against an ace.

CHART B-4   BASIC STRATEGY FOR FOUR OR MORE DECKS

YOUR HAND	DEALER'S UP CARD									
	2	3	4	5	6	7	8	9	10	ACE
8	H	H	H	H	H	H	H	H	H	H
9	H	D	D	D	D	H	H	H	H	H
10	D	D	D	D	D	D	D	D	H	H
11	D	D	D	D	D	D	D	D	D	H
12	H	H	S	S	S	H	H	H	H	H
13	S	S	S	S	S	H	H	H	H	H
14	S	S	S	S	S	H	H	H	H	H
15	S	S	S	S	S	H	H	H	H	H
16	S	S	S	S	S	H	H	H	H	H
17	S	S	S	S	S	S	S	S	S	S
A2	H	H	H	D	D	H	H	H	H	H
A3	H	H	H	D	D	H	H	H	H	H
A4	H	H	D	D	D	H	H	H	H	H
A5	H	H	D	D	D	H	H	H	H	H
A6	H	D	D	D	D	H	H	H	H	H
A7	S	D	D	D	D	S	S	H	H	H
A8	S	S	S	S	S	S	S	S	S	S
A9	S	S	S	S	S	S	S	S	S	S
AA	SP	SP	SP	SP	SP	SP	SP	SP	SP	SP
22	H	H	SP	SP	SP	SP	H	H	H	H
33	H	H	SP	SP	SP	SP	H	H	H	H
66	H	SP	SP	SP	SP	H	H	H	H	H
77	SP	SP	SP	SP	SP	SP	H	H	H	H
88	SP	SP	SP	SP	SP	SP	SP	SP	SP	SP
99	SP	SP	SP	SP	SP	S	SP	SP	S	S
1010	S	S	S	S	S	S	S	S	S	S

H - HIT   S- STAND   D - DOUBLE   SP - SPLIT

Exceptional situations for Table B-4 are given on the next page.

CHART B-4   EXCEPTIONAL SITUATIONS

If your two card total is 8 or less, always HIT. If you have
4,4,consider it as 8. If you have 5,5, consider it as 10.

If the casino allows doubling down _after_ pair splitting the
following changes in basic strategy apply:

> Split 2,2 or 3, 3 vs. a dealer's 2 or 3.
> Split 4,4 vs. a dealer's 5 or 6.
> Split 6,6 vs. a dealer's 2.

If the casino allows SURRENDER (the option to throw in your
original two-card hand and give up half of your bet) then you
would surrender a 15 or 16 against a dealer's 10-value card or
Ace as indicated on page 12.

Basic Strategy for Two Decks

The basic strategy for two decks is identical to the strategy for
four or more decks given above. All the plays are the same except
for the following:

> With a hand of 9 double down against a dealer's 2.
> With a hand of 7,4 or 6,5 double down against a dealer's ACE.

How to Learn the Basic Strategy

I advise that you learn the basic strategy for multiple
decks (Chart B-4) first. You will be using this strategy most
often since most of the casinos in the world use four decks. You
can learn the few differences in strategy between single and multiple
decks later on. Many accomplished players use the multiple deck
strategy in all games including single deck games. This is a
sound practice since the differences between strategies are so
slight that in terms of percentages one loses only a few one-
hundredths of one percent in advantage when one uses the multiple
deck strategy in a single deck game.

The multiple deck strategy is more conservative than the
single deck strategy. With the multiple deck strategy you double
down less often and you split pairs less often. You hit more rather
than doubling or splitting. Because of such conservatism the
multiple deck strategy is safer to use against dealers who are
potential cheats. A player risks less money with the multiple deck
strategy because he doubles and splits less often. This is another
important reason for using the multiple deck strategy in single or
double deck games. Protection from being cheated always far
outweighs any mathematical advantage the player may be giving up.

In learning the charts you must first understand how to read
them. The numbers indicated along the top of the chart represent
every card   the dealer could have as his "up card" (the card that
is face up on the table). In playing basic strategy you always play
in relation to the dealer's up card. The numbers along the left
hand side of the charts represent the player's hands. These are
made up of two cards where doubling and pair splitting are indicated. Where hitting is indicated the player's card total may be
composed of more than two cards. For example, in Chart B-4, your
hand is 15 and the dealer's up card is a 10, it say to HIT. If
your 15 is made up of two cards, 9 and 6 or 10 and 5, you would hit
it. But you would also hit any 15 even if it was made up of a 2
and a 10 and a 3 or any other combination of two or more cards adding
up to 15.

The charts are easy to read. Simply go down along the left hand side to find the player's hand that you want, then go across the page from the player's hand and then straight up to the dealer's up card. Where the player's hand intersects with the dealer's up card is indicated the correct play. You have four types of plays: hit, stand, double your bet, or split a pair (if you are dealt a pair).

In learning the charts it is quickest if you actually get a deck of cards and play blackjack at home. Keep the chart beside you on the table and refer to it while practising. Always guess the correct play first _then_ check your play by looking at the chart. It takes most players between 6 and 48 hours of practice to memorize the basic strategy well enough to play it perfectly in a casino.

Learning the basic strategy is the most difficult part of learning to win for most players. Yet the strategy is not a hard thing to learn, it is just tedious. Keep this piece of advice in mind. Say to yourself:
IF I LEARN THE BASIC STRATEGY, THE REST WILL BE FAIRLY EASY.

Therefore, if you can muster up enough courage to learn the basic strategy you will be well on your way to becoming a good blackjack player.

Here are two further suggestions to help you learn the basic strategy.
(1) Make a wallet-size copy of the basic strategy. If you like colors, color-code the chart, using different colors for hitting, standing, etc. Carry the chart with you wherever you go.
(2) Ask yourself practice questions to test yourself on the basic strategy. For example, 12 vs. 2, do I hit? Answer, then check your chart. 9 vs. 3, do I hit? Answer, then check your chart. This question-asking is technically called the INQUIRY METHOD OF INSTRUCTION by education specialists. It is the quickest and most powerful method

by which to learn anything. The method forces you to think
and makes it difficult for you to forget what you have already
learned. Always use it.

Use the inquiry method to practise the hands given in
the Practice Table below. The table contains almost every hand
you will ever get in a blackjack game. In each column the
player's hand is on the left and the dealer's up card on the
right (Our thanks to Lawrence Revere for the idea of the table).

PRACTICE TABLE

A7 4	A9 3	A9 6	A7 5	14 A	A7 6	A9 5
99 2	99 A	99 4	99 6	99 3	99 7	92 8
65 4	74 5	92 6	83 3	16 4	14 9	15 A
15 9	13 A	16 A	16 9	A5 3	83 X	99 5
A7 A	77 6	77 8	77 3	77 5	77 4	77 2
16 X	16 3	16 6	14 X	74 2	15 X	A5 4
A5 5	A5 6	A3 5	A3 6	16 7	A3 3	53 3
14 8	15 7	14 7	15 8	A9 4	16 8	72 6
72 3	54 8	63 5	54 2	72 7	63 4	66 4
88 X	66 7	66 3	66 5	66 2	66 6	15 3
A6 3	A3 5	A8 2	A8 4	A8 6	A8 3	22 2
22 8	22 6	22 5	22 3	22 7	22 4	65 7
74 A	83 9	82 6	73 A	A4 2	55 7	A4 6
14 5	14 3	15 2	15 4	15 6	16 5	13 4
44 3	62 5	44 2	88 9	44 5	44 4	A7 2
A4 4	A6 6	A6 4	A6 5	A7 3	A6 2	33 6
33 5	33 3	33 7	33 2	33 4	33 8	A8 5
13 3	15 5	13 5	14 6	14 4	13 6	13 8
AA 2	AA X	AA 7	AA 8	AA A	AA 9	44 6
55 2	64 X	82 4	73 8	64 5	73 3	10 9
A2 6	A4 3	A4 5	A2 5	A2 3	A2 4	14 2
16 2	12 4	12 3	13 2	12 5	12 2	AA 3
53 5	53 6	A7 X	44 7	62 6	53 4	12 6

6   LEARNING TO COUNT CARDS

Why must one learn to keep track of cards? Because computer studies by Professor Thorp and Julian Braun have shown that the player who uses basic strategy wins more hands than the dealer when a lot of small cards have been dealt out of the deck. Thus, when you, the player know you are about to win more hands than the dealer in the next few upcoming hands, you would bet more money than usual and show a profit in the long run by betting in this way. Conversely, when more small cards, than large cards, are left inside the deck the dealer wins more hands. In this situation you the player will bet the minimum bet or stop playing.

What are small cards? The most important small cards are the 3's, 4's, 5's and 6's. What are the large cards? The important large cards are all the cards that are worth ten in the game: the tens, jacks, queens, and kings. No other cards need to be kept track of. How do I keep track of the small cards? Every time you see a small card out of the deck, count it as a plus one (+1). Keep a running count of all the small cards as you see them. How do I count the ten-value cards? Count each ten-value card as a minus one (-1). Keep a running count of these large cards along with the small cards. The rule is that each +1 cancels out each -1 as you are counting. Thus, if you see two small cards and count them you have a running count of +2 (+1 added to +1). Should you see one large card next, you count it -1 and subtract this -1 from the +2. This mental operation will leave you with a net running count of +1. Such a running count must be kept from the time the dealer begins dealing to the time that he finishes dealing.

Whenever your net count is plus you should place a larger bet on your next hand because you have the advantage. When your net count is zero or minus bet your minimum wager. The count described is sometimes referred to as the HI-OPT count. This count is the simplest and most accurate count devised to date. (A special strategy was constructed for the HI-OPT count. The HI-OPT STRATEGY is an advanced and very powerful playing strategy that a player should

learn after he has proven to himself that he can win in a casino.
The HI-OPT STRATEGY will give the player twice the long term
advantage that he has using basic strategy. Information about the
HI-OPT STRATEGY is contained in the centerfold of this volume).

The HI-OPT count is shown on the following page. Use the
page to practice the count at first, before practicing with a deck
of cards. Be sure you understand which cards count +1, which count
-1, and which count 0.

The HI-OPT count is very easy to learn. Most players can master
it in about 30 minutes by practising with a single deck. You may
want to learn it before tackling the basic strategy since the basic
strategy takes hours to learn. You may also study both the count
and the basic strategy at the same time. Learning to keep the count
accurately is more important than playing accurately (with basic strategy). This is so because if you have had any experience at all
with the game of blackjack you probably already know the basics of
basic strategy. The count is more important because it signals you
when to raise the size of your bets. However, optimum play requires
both accurate basic strategy and accurate tracking of cards.
Although this will take a few hours of practice you definitely do not
need a mathematical mind to learn to win as the casinos would have
you believe. Learn at home, practise by yourself or with friends,
keep records of your wins and losses. And you will see within a few
hours of play how easy it is to win.

HI-OPT COUNT

CARD VALUE	2	3	4	5	6	7	8	9	10	Ace
POINT COUNT	0	+1	+1	+1	+1	0	0	0	-1	0

PRACTICE CARD COMBINATIONS

Cards		Net Count	Cards		Net Count	Cards		Net Count
2,3	=	+1	2,3,4	=	+2	2,3,4,5	=	+3
3,4	=	+2	3,4,5	=	+3	3,4,5,6	=	+4
4,5	=	+2	4,5,6	=	+3	4,5,6,7	=	+3
5,6	=	+2	5,6,7	=	+2	5,6,7,8	=	+2
6,7	=	+1	6,7,8	=	+1	6,7,8,9	=	+1
7,8	=	0	7,8,9	=	0	7,8,9,10	=	-1
8,9	=	0	8,9,10	=	-1	8,9,10,A	=	-1
9,10	=	-1	9,10,A	=	-1	9,10,A,2	=	-1
10,A	=	-1	10,A,2	=	-1	10,10,A,A	=	-2
3,10	=	0	A,2,3	=	+1	10,10,3,4	=	0
4,10	=	0	A,3,4	=	+2	10,A,2,3	=	0
5,10	=	0	A,7,8	=	0	A,2,3,4	=	+2
6,10	=	0	2,7,8	=	0	10,10,10,A	=	-3

If you do not understand how the net counts were derived ask someone to help you. You must understand this page to know the HI-OPT count.

INSURANCE

Insurance is an optional bet that is offered in most casinos in the world. Insurance is offered in only one special case. Whenever the dealer's up card is an ACE, the dealer will ask the players whether they want to buy insurance. What this proposition means is that he wants to bet you the player whether he has a ten-value card underneath the ACE or not. That is, you can take out some extra money and bet him that he does in fact, have a ten-value card underneath his ACE. If he does have a ten-value card then you will win your insurance bet. The payoff for an insurance bet is two to one. That is, if you bet one dollar, you will win two dollars, you get three dollars back altogether. The player is allowed to buy insurance only up to half the amount of his original bet. For example, if you have a ten dollar bet up and the dealer deals himself an ACE, you can buy only five dollars worth of insurance, which is half of your original bet. But you have to find another five dollars with which to buy insurance, that is, you can't take any money away from your original bet. As was said initially, the insurance is an extra optional bet that you can make.

Is the insurance bet a profitable bet for the player? In general, the insurance bet is not a good bet for the player, unless the player is keeping a count of cards. If you are keeping a count of cards, using the HI-OPT Count, then the insurance bet becomes profitable when the TRUE COUNT is plus 2 or higher. With a count of plus 2 we know that there are two extra ten-value cards, in relation to small cards, in the deck. When this is the case, the dealer will in fact have a ten-value card underneath his ACE more than 33% of the time. And since the payoff is two to one, this is the time that it is profitable to take insurance. Notice that you always take insurance according to the TRUE COUNT. When playing against a single deck at the top of the deck you need a count of plus two or more to take insurance. However, if there is only about half a deck left, all you need is a count of plus one, in order to take insurance. This is so because at the half-deck level, you divide the running count by a half in order to get the TRUE COUNT.

Thus, a running count of plus one divided by half is a TRUE COUNT
of plus two. In the same way, when playing against four decks,
in order to get the TRUE COUNT you would divide your running count
by four. Therefore, if you just began to play against four decks,
the running count would have to be +8 in order for you to take
insurance. This is so, because +8 divided by 4 is +2. If you are
playing against four decks and one deck has been dealt out, leaving
3 decks, then your running count should be plus 6 before you can
take insurance. In the same way, against two decks, your running
count needs to be plus four or higher for you to take insurance.

Many players and most dealers will advise the player to take
insurance whenever he has a blackjack. They say you cannot lose in
this way. The advice to take insurance whenever you have a blackjack
is wrong. Whether you take insurance or not has nothing to do with
whether you have a blackjack or not in your hand. You always consider
insurance to be a separate bet. You only take insurance when the
TRUE COUNT is plus two or higher, no matter what your hand is. It is
that simple. Don't let anyone confuse you by telling you to always
insure a blackjack. They are right to a degree, that you cannot
lose if you insure a blackjack. However, what they do not know is
that you can win more in the longrun by not insuring a blackjack if
the count is less than plus two.

Taking insurance as recommended above can add up to approximately half a percent to your overall advantage. This is a substantial advantage in the game of blackjack. Therefore, it is important for you to take insurance whenever the opportunity arises.

7   THE SHOE GAME

The optimum method of playing against four, five, six
or more decks dealt out of a shoe will now be described.

Step 1

The first thing to do is to find out whether all the
cards are in the shoe. This can be done by using a simple plus-
minus count. Count 3's to 7's plus one each. Count ten value
cards and aces as minus one each. Simply stand back from the
table and wait until the dealer starts dealing from a fresh shoe.
Begin counting and count right until the time he hits the plastic
separator card and stops dealing. Make a note of the count that
you are left with then repeat the whole operation again, twice.
Then add up the three final counts that you have. They should add
up to approximately zero. If your net figure is a plus figure,
like plus 4 or more, then you can be suspicious that some tens or
aces are missing from the shoe. Don't play at that table. Go
to another table and repeat the counting operation. Better still,
leave that casino and go to another one.

Step 2

Once you are satisfied that all the cards are in the shoe,
the next thing to observe is how the dealer picks up the cards and
how he shuffles the cards. Again, you are still not playing. You
are only standing back watching the other players play. As far
as picking the cards up, he should pick the cards up from right
to left all in one sweeping motion, or from left to right in the
same kind of sweeping motion. He should leave each player's cards
together when they are picked up. He should not pick up one player's
cards who's sitting in the middle, then another player's cards who's
sitting on one side, and then another's cards on the other side, and
so on. If he is doing anything like this, then simply leave the
table or leave the casino. What he is doing is stacking the cards.

Once you're satisfied that the cards are being picked up properly, then watch how he shuffles the cards. Make sure that the cards are well-shuffled and that they are all thoroughly shuffled with the first half of the deck shuffled into the second half, and the first quarter of the deck shuffled into the fourth quarter, and so on. Most dealers shuffle in one prescribed way and it is a good thorough shuffle. I have never seen a dealer deviate from the standard type of shuffle in a four deck game. However, some dealers shuffle more thoroughly than others. A thorough shuffle is best for the player.

Step 3

Now that you have determined that you are in a honest game you may sit down. But before you sit down, just wait until he starts dealing from a fresh shoe again and get the count. Don't sit down until the count is a plus count. Why sit down at a negative count? You might as well wait until you get the advantage. Then sit down and bet your maximum bet. This is fairly neat but don't expect to get away with it more than once in any casino on any one day. You can get away with it but the dealer and pit boss will be watching you pretty closely as you play. It is simply not worth the risk of getting barred by engaging in this tactic too often.

Step 4

This is the final step. It deals with wagering. Complete wagering and money management instructions for all deck levels are given in the chapter titled METHODS OF WAGERING. Please refer to that chapter. Other details pertaining to the shoe game will be found throughout the book under appropriate headings. Therefore, we are not finished with the shoe game. This chapter should have taught you how to approach the shoe game.

8   CHEATING IN LAS VEGAS

Before Edward Thorp's Beat the Dealer was published in
1962 the question in relation to cheating was "Do they cheat in
Las Vegas?" Since the publication of Professor Thorp's book
there has been much evidence of cheating in Las Vegas, in Reno
and in Lake Tahoe, as well as in other casinos in the world.
The more important question today is not "Do they cheat in Las
Vegas?" but rather "How much do they cheat in Nevada and in other
casinos in the world?" The evidence for cheating will now be
presented. The evidence will be limited to Nevada casinos since
this is where 90% of all the blackjack action is in the world.

The Las Vegas SUN and REVIEW-JOURNAL report arrests and convictions of Cheating Blackjack Dealers

Quite frequently the two Las Vegas newspapers report
the arrests of cheating blackjack dealers in Nevada casinos by
the Gaming Control Board. The dealers are usually charged with
"dealing from other than the top of the deck." The dealers are
usually fined several hundred, or sometimes, a few thousand dollars
and are fired by the casino. The casino always denies any knowledge of the fact that the dealer was cheating. In some cases the
casino is telling the truth, in other cases the casino is not
telling the truth. On the following pages are accounts of dealers
being charged with cheating. These accounts are taken from Nevada
newspapers.

CHEATED AT '21'

LAS VEGAS SUN, August 29, 1974, page 11

CARSON CITY (UPI) - The Nevada Gaming Control
Board has filed a complaint against
          , owner of the Owl Club in Yerington,
alleging he cheated customers in his "21"
game in July and August.

The Control Board asks that the gaming license
of   be revoked and he be fined $10,000.
Mulderick has 15 days to answer the complaint.

The board said its undercover agents discovered
          peeking at the cards in the deck and
dealing "seconds" in the game on more than five
occasions between July 26 and August 15.

The State Gaming Commission last week issued an
emergency order closing the games and slot
machines.

TONOPAH CASINOS SHUT BY GAMING AUTHORITIES
Las Vegas SUN, Tuesday June 11, 1974, page 9.

Carson City (UPI) - The Nevada Gaming Commission
has closed down the gambling at two Tonopah
casinos because of alleged cheating and other irregularities, it was announced Monday.

Philip Hannifin, chairman of the State Gaming
Control Board, said the Commission granted a
board petition to close the table games, seal the
slot machines and pull the gaming licences of the
Tonopah Club and the Tonopah Belle.

The board petition for emergency closure followed
seven months of surveillance by gaming agents
he said.

The board alleged dealers looked at their hole
card when neither an ace nor a 10-value card was
face up, peeked in various fashions at the
unused portion of the deck, and dealt "seconds"
- that is, other than the top card.

Dr. Humble and Friends Lose Out on $3,000,000

Some of my former students who I've taught to play winning blackjack and I have pooled skills and managed to win slightly in excess of $300,000 playing blackjack in the last few years, mainly in Las Vegas casinos. We should have won in excess of $3,000,000 according to the mathematical advantage that our strategy had. We are very good players, therefore, the below par earnings cannot be the result of making a lot of playing mistakes. We were rarely shuffled up on. And we played a lot of our sessions against the shoe. Furthermore, we did win at the expected mathematical rate when playing in games in Toronto. Therefore, there is only one explanation left for why we did not win the amount of money we should have won. That explanation is dealer cheating.

Mobbed-Up Dealers

According to a recent interview with an individual who is high up in the hierarchy of organized crime, the mob has dealers placed in almost every casino in the state of Nevada. These dealers help the mob take money out of the casinos by allowing certain other mobsters to win money while playing at their table. In order to balance the chips on the table, the dealers turn around and cheat honest players like you and me. In the interview quoted below, taken from the 1976 January-February edition of the Rouge et Noir Newsletter published in New York, we see direct evidence for this kind of cheating.

The interview is on the next two pages.

ORGANIZED CRIME AND CASINO GAMING

AN INTERVIEW

Knowledge of the intimate details of Organized Crime's
current activities, in the world of casino gaming,
is limited to a handful of individuals. Our interview-
ee is one of these individuals, as you will find from
the information he has provided.

To what extent is organized crime active in Nevada
casino gaming?

I have difficulty with that question because the term
organized crime means different things to different
people. Rather than get caught up in a philosophical
discussion, let me say that the elements that were
represented by previous owners are still active in
Nevada casino gaming.

Let me explain that further. Our people may have sold
hotel-casino operations, but we have our people in key
spots.

We're primarily interested in the areas of casino
credit issuance and collection, junkets and the supervision of table games.

Why the interest in supervision of blackjack games?

Blackjack provides one of our biggest and safest
sources of income. We have trained card counters who
are "allowed" to play for large stakes without being
barred. It isn't necessary for us to cheat. The decks
don't get shuffled-up as often for our players, and
house personnel don't over-react to large increases
in our bet size.

The scam is so simple and effective that we've spawned
a bevy of competitors. So many insiders now have
working arrangements with card counters that it has
become necessary to bar unaffiliated counters to
protect the bottom line performance. Unfortunately,
the "boys" are getting too greedy for their own good.

What do you see as Organized Crime's future in Nevada?

Casino gaming is small potatoes compared to sports
betting. Our long range plan is to become more active
in the promotion of sports events in Nevada.

We're particularly anxious to feature events of national interest wherein we promote the event, and house the participants. When we can house, feed and entertain the "cast", the results can be affected in any number of ways without anyone becoming wiser.

When we want to throw a participant off we can offer sex of the quality and quantity that is hard to refuse; the room can become uncomfortable and/or noisy; subliminal techniques are being tried; food can be doctored, etc. We don't have to balance the betting books on such operations, and the acquiescence of participants is not required.

I don't have to spell out how we use casinos in influencing participants in non-area sports events. You are smart enough to figure it out for yourself.

END OF INTERVIEW

It should be noticed that the person interviewed
said that winning money from mobbed up blackjack dealers has
been the most lucrative method for obtaining money for the
mob from the casinos. By lucrative the person means millions
of dollars. In order to recover this money, honest players will
have had to have been cheated out of millions of dollars. How
else can the blackjack tables show a profit "on the bottom line"
as he claims they do? The dealers must be cheating even though
he says they don't have to cheat.

Player-dealer partnerships are corroborated in Mike
Goodman's 1975 book "Your Best Bet". Mr. Goodman, a veteran pit
boss in Las Vegas says on page 35 of his book:

> "The ideal setup, one that counters and cheaters
> dream about, is talking a dealer into becoming a
> partner. It's happening more and more as the
> gambling business continues to mushroom. Reliable
> casino employees are becoming much harder to find.
> In Nevada, it's safe to say that almost every large
> casino is being victimized by one or more dealers
> who are working with agents on the other side of
> the table."

Mr. Goodman goes on to say, "Even today there's no telling
how much leakage or cheating is going on in clubs still using single
decks." (Page 3).

I was lucky enough to observe such a skimming operation at the
Stilton recently. I was strolling by looking for a good table at
about 10:30 one morning and I see this guy sitting in the middle of
the table. The guy was in his fifties, balding with grey hair,
smoking a cigar and wearing a blue shirt with white polka dots.
He was smiling and drinking, a sportsman type having a good time.
I saw he was playing three hands at $500 a hand, black chips. I also
saw that he had about $8000 worth of black chips in front of him.
This was very interesting to observe. In fact I wasn't the only one
interested. A crowd started to gather around this player. I asked
how long he had been playing and the young fellow beside me said

that he had bought one thousand dollars worth of chips about twenty minutes ago. I stood there and I watched. Then I looked up at the dealer. I didn't believe my eyes. The dealer he was playing against was a dealer I had been playing against off and on for four years in this casino and I had never won against him! This morning the dealer couldn't do anything right. He was busting about four out of five times! I watched the player play to see how good he was. The man was playing fairly good basic strategy. I also watched the cards to keep count to see if he was counting. He wasn't counting. He was betting big money sometimes when the count was positive and other times he was betting big money when the count was negative. To make a long story short, I waited until he quit. He quit about 45 minutes later and cashed more than $31,000 worth of chips. The dealer was smiling the whole time, also have a good time. The pit boss was there watching things. He was also very happy about the whole operation. I'm sure that the pit boss was in on this skimming operation. The pit boss is almost always involved in such operations because it is the pit boss's job not to allow any player who is not one of the "boys" to win any appreciable amount of money. When someone does win a lot of money quickly, and he's not supposed to, the pit bosses get very, very upset. Exactly the opposite reactions were observed on this occasion.

If you ever see such a situation and there are some spaces open to place bets on, just go right ahead, sit down and start betting. It's an easy way to win some money. Over the years I have observed similar skims in several Las Vegas casinos but I did not realize that they were skims then. I thought the players simply got lucky. I realize now that you can't get lucky against any cheating dealer on the Las Vegas Strip.

International Blackjack Club Exposes Unsafe Casinos

The Club surveys players using winning strategies in order to discover which casinos are unsafe. Players using the HI-OPT and other winning strategies are mailed a survey form which asks them to state how many times they won and how many times they lost in each casino they played in. The results are compiled into a table. The casinos are ranked from best to worst according to the total numberof wins against losses. The summary table reveals that winning players do not win very often in certain casinos. The dealers in these casinos are doing things that the dealers in the safe casinos are not doing. The summary table provides indirect but scientific evidence of foul play. The table is reproduced in this volume as Table P in the chapter titled PLAYING CONDITIONS IN SPECIFIC CASINOS.

Professor Humble Observes Cheating

I have observed cheating on a number of occasions in Las Vegas. On one occasion my friend David Brucher and I caught a dealer stacking the cards in a shoe game. We caught him arranging the cards in a high-low sequence as he was picking them up. It looked slow and unusual because the common method of picking up cards is in one motion from right to left. This stacking was observed in the Backbeam casino.

On another occasion Nick Barreta and I caught a female dealer dealing herself aces. This happened in the Regal Laxative casino. There were four of us at the table. I came in late and sat next to third base. The other three players, including Nick, were grumbling because they were losing. They began making fun of the dealer. She was young but homely. One of the players said her chest would make a good surf board. She got red in the face but said nothing. She gathered up the cards, shuffled several times, dealt and came up with the ace of diamonds as her up card. She asked for insurance, no one took it, she didn't have it. As soon as we all played our hands she reshuffled, instead of dealing two more roundsas she used to, and again dealt herself the ace of diamonds.

She didn't have blackjack this time either. As soon as we played
our hands she reshuffled and guess what card she dealt herself
this time? Right. The ace of diamonds for a third time! This
time she had a ten underneath for a blackjack. We all stood
up in one motion and left the casino. Moral? A dealer's chest
should never be likened to a surfboard.

On another occasion Doe and I were staying and playing
at the Sombrera. It was late so I went to bed. Doe stayed. As
I walked into the casino area the next morning who do I see but
my friend Doe. He had been playing all night. He was down about
$8,000. He was playing against a single deck. The reason he de-
cided to play all night was because the dealer was showing him
both the burn card and the bottom card every time he shuffled and
because the dealer dealt out all the cards. I tried to get my
friend to quit because he did look tired. Doe wanted to get even.
I thought the situation over and decided to help him win by sitting
down, playing myself, and watching his play to correct any mistakes.
Doe was not making mistakes. His count was the same as mine and
his betting was accurate most of the time. I lost $500 in about
20 minutes. Doe lost another $1200. I realized that George the
dealer was cheating us. I was so mad I said, "George, stop cheating".
George smiled then laughed at me. I quit. We were definitely cheated
by George because it was impossible for us, especially for Doe, to
lose that much money with the advantage we had. Our strategy was
the most powerful that money could buy up to that time. We had won
in excess of $90,000 with it playing in private games in our home
town. For your protection I can tell you that George is very tall,
on the slim side, wears glasses, has long greyish-black hair which
is puffed out at the sides and combed back. He now deals a shoe
game at the Strand.

Ten Off The Top

A very common cheating practice is for the dealer to deal
himself a ten-value card right after the shuffle. This move is
fairly easy to learn and gives the dealer a large percentage advantage

over the players. A mathematics professor actually went around from casino to casino and counted the number of times the dealer came up with a ten, jack, queen or king immediately after the shuffle. He found that it occured over 40% of the time. It should have happened only 31% of the time because there are 16 ten-value cards in a deck of 52, which comes to 31%. Need we say more? The professor reported this finding at the Second Annual Conference on Gambling which was held in Lake Tahoe in May, 1975. This professor is an excellent blackjack player. Yet he is no longer able to win anywhere in the state of Nevada because he is known to the casino personnel. The professor also stated at the Conference that he does not recommend that anyone play blackjack in the state of Nevada. (This professor's name is NOT Thorp.)

Another professor reported at the same Conference that he played head-on in a two-deck game in a Strip casino and lost every single hand through the deck. This professor was a Negro.

No Shuffle

Another common way that the dealers have of cheating has to do with shuffling. Many Strip dealers do not shuffle the deck very thoroughly. Some dealers will only shuffle the deck twice then deal after the cut. This is one way of stacking the cards in a high-low sequence. In this case the dealer takes advantage of the way black-jack players play their hands. That is, by not shuffling much he preserves the order of the cards as they were played. And this is usually a high-low sequence rather than a random distribution. The result is that the players get a lot of stiffs dealt to them.

A Demonstration

If you wish a demonstration of cheating moves you may purchase one for as little as $50. A friend and I did this in Las Vegas. Through a third party we got a dealer to come up to our hotel room to show us what he could do. He "showed" us how he dealt seconds, thirds, fourths and bottoms. My eyes were about 10 inches away from the deck in his hands yet I could not see that he was cheating. It looked as though every card was coming off the top of the deck.

       Mr. Lawrence Revere, a professional who teaches blackjack in Las Vegas, also gave a demonstration of seconds to my friend Doe and me when we were taking lessons from him several years ago.

9   THE DEALER

If I was asked to select the most important chapters in
this book I would select this chapter on the Dealer and the next
two: How to Spot the Cheating Dealer and Dealing with the Dealer.
The honesty of the dealer is critical to winning. No matter how
powerful your strategy or how much of a mathematical genius you
may be, you will not win against a cheating dealer. The purpose
of this chapter is to discuss different kinds of dealers. How to
recognize them and how to play against them. I begin by talking
about the most important kind of dealer: the cheating dealer.

The Cheating Dealer

First, let's learn how the cheating dealer cheats.

The most common way of cheating is by the use of sleight
of hand. By sleight of hand is meant the use of manual dexterity
to manipulate cards and deal cards from other than the top of the deck.
The most common type of sleight in casino blackjack is the dealing of
seconds, which means dealing the second card from the top of the
deck, while leaving the top card intact. Thus, what the dealer is
doing (while he is adjusting his chips or paying players off, or
while he's looking underneath his up card when it is a ten or an ace to
see whether he has a ten or an ace underneath) is moving the deck
around at different angles and it is on these occasions that he has
a chance to crimp the top card and take a peek at it. Now, once he
knows what the top card is then he'll know whether he needs to deal
seconds or not in order to save himself the top card so that he'll
make his hand.

Most dealers who can deal seconds can also deal bottoms.
That is dealing the card from the bottom of the deck. Many dealers
can also deal thirds and fourths. That is, the third or fourth card
from the top of the deck. In large and in small casinos alike, these

sleight of hand dealers are so expert that it is impossible to
detect when they are dealing seconds or cheating you in other ways.
Therefore, don't waste your time trying to spot such cheating.
Learn to detect cheating in other ways, as described in this book.

Another common way of cheating is to stack the cards.
Cards may be stacked in a number of ways. The two most common ways
are to arrange the discards in a certain order as they are being
picked up or to set up the cards in a desired position while they
are being shuffled. In casino blackjack it is rare that you'll see
the dealer picking up the discards in a seemingly random order or
in an order that is haphazard, such as a high card, then a low card,
then a high card, then a low card. The way dealers are trained to
pick up cards in a casino are from left to right or from right to
left, all in one sweep, keeping the cards for each player's hand
together so that the hand may be reconstructed at a later time should
the player dispute the dealer's call as to whether he won or lost
the hand.

It is rare that you'll see a dealer picking up the cards in
any other way other than in a smooth order from his left to right,
or from right to left. However, a fellow player and I did spot a
dealer picking up the cards and arranging them in a high-low stack
in a four deck game in a Las Vegas Strip casino.

In addition to stacking the cards, there are other ways to
cheat with the shoe. One way which has been used by casinos is to
simply take some tens and/or aces out of the shoe. This automatically
raises the casino's advantage. Another way to cheat is to use a
HOLD-OUT shoe. This is a shoe that holds the top card in place so
that the second card can be dealt (seconds) and the top card saved
by the dealer for his own hand. A man in Las Vegas makes and sells
these shoes. He gave one of my former students a demonstration. It
is impossible for the average player to recognize this shoe. It is
different only in one respect from the honest shoe. The face plate
(which has the hole in it) is about one quarter of an inch higher.

In this way the dealer can get a peek of the top card from behind.
You may detect such a shoe in the way the dealer pushes out the
cards. In this shoe in order to hold the top card he must hold it
steady through the hole with one finger while pulling out the
second card from the bottom slit with another finger. The tell-
tale sign is a dealer using two fingers to deal but only one
finger is moving. At the Second Annual Conference on Gambling a
verteran gambler told us that there was a special dealers' school
in Las Vegas where dealers learned how to cheat with the shoe.

A general statement about cheating comes from a former
casino owner, Harold Smith Jr. He states in his book <u>I Want To</u>
<u>Quit Winners</u>, "We could cheat all the time and they would never know
it. We're far more expert at this business than they are." By
"they" Mr. Smith is referring to the agents of the Gaming Control
Board, who are supposed to be experts at detecting cheating. If
Mr. Smith's statement is true how can the average player ever hope
to spot cheating?

There are many other ways in which the dealer can cheat,
but they are all variations on those mentioned above. The important
thing to learn is how to spot a potentially cheating dealer or how
to detect the fact that you are being cheated without actually seeing
it. We now turn to this topic.

10   HOW TO SPOT THE CHEATING DEALER

There are a number of ways to spot the potentially cheating dealer.

The No Bust Dealer

A dealer who seldom busts is probably cheating. He deals himself no-bust hands by using seconds. One female player playing on the Strip at my table said, "Don't you ever bust?" The dealer just smiled. The dealers in Downtown Las Vegas bust more often than the Strip dealers. It is easy to see the contrast by playing on the Strip then jumping into a taxi and speeding to a Downtown casino to play. You will see that the difference between the two types of dealers is as great as the difference between night and day.

Jewelry

Another tell-tale sign of some cheating dealers is the wearing of expensive rings. These rings are usually studded with diamonds. Some of them have a ruby in the middle or other precious gems. Middle-aged female dealers usually have diamond studded rings, while cheating male dealers, both middle-aged and older, have gold rings studded with diamonds and other precious stones. When you watch those dealers' hands dealing it becomes obvious that they did not purchase their rings by working hard and being honest.

Time-Watching

Another sign of a cheating dealer is the dealer who is always turning his wrist in order to check the time. The dealer usually does this in order to take a peek at the deck in his hand. Dealers work 40 minute shifts, then they have a twenty minute break and then come back for another 40 minute shift. The dealers have such a fine sense of time they could tell you what time it is to an accuracy of a few minutes without even looking at their watches. There is no need for them to keep looking at what time it is every few minutes. They're not going any where anyway. Are they? Always avoid a wrist twister.

Empty Table

Another very good sign of a cheating dealer is a dealer
who is standing behind an empty table. Usually this is a cheating
dealer who has cleaned out all the players at the table and keeps
on cleaning out new players that sit at his table. They lose all
their money and leave. Thus, he is left with an empty table. I
have found this to be particularly true at the five dollar minimum
tables in Downtown Las Vegas, in Lake Tahoe, and in Reno. These
tables are usually empty. I've also noticed that the dealers at
such tables are always older than the dealers at the one dollar
tables in the same casino.

The $100 minimum and the $25 minimum tables

One hundred and twenty-five dollar minimum tables are traps
for the unwary player. These tables contain cheating dealers almost
one hundred per cent of the time. Such tables are most often found
on the Las Vegas Strip. The five dollar minimum table in Downtown
Las Vegas discussed above is analogous to the $25 table on the Strip.

Dealer-Big Winner Combination

You have probably seen, on occasion, a blackjack player
betting $500 or a $1000 a hand and playing several hands or even
all seven hands at the table. When you see such a situation and you
see that the player has been winning and has thousands of dollars
worth of chips in front of him, the chances are approximately 100%
that he is working with a cheating dealer and skimming money from
the casino. Take a good look at the dealer in this situation and
remember him.

An Honest Dealer: The Novice

The novice or apprentice dealer is the only dealer that
you can be positive about in terms of his honesty. This kind of
dealer is very easy to recognize because there is an older more

experienced dealer standing right beside him at the table. The
older dealer is watching the novice deal and giving him pointers
on how to pick up the cards, how to pay off the players, how to
shuffle, etc. This is a counter's dream whenever he sees one of
these dealers. These dealers are most plentiful in Downtown Las
Vegas and also in Reno. They are rarely found on the Las Vegas
Strip, although I did find one such dealer, a Negro chap, learning
to deal at a $2.00 minimum table at the Stilton in 1975. He still
deals at the same table. But he is no longer a novice. When you
spot a novice dealer run right over to the table and start betting
your money. I have done this every single time that I have been
lucky enough to find such a dealer and I have won in approximately
80% of the sittings.

A Sign of Honesty: Money on the Table

A very good sign of an honest dealer (or more precisely,
of a dealer that is dealing honestly at this particular time) is
the fact that the players have a lot of chips in front of them at
his table. That is, what I'm advising you to do here is to look
for a table at which the players are winning money. This will be a
table at which either the dealer is an honest dealer who has been
busting a lot recently, or a table at which the dealer may be dis-
honest but for some reason is dealing honestly and busting a lot
of times at this particular time. I should add though that you will
find it difficult to find a seat at such a table. The same is true
for the novice dealer's table. Once players start to win the
tables become filled up very quickly. This "money on the table"
angle was told to me by an old-time dealer in 1973 who used to deal
at the Sombrera. He doesn't deal there anymore and I haven't seen
him dealing anywhere. I wonder what happened to good old Dash?

The guidelines given in this chapter are critical to winning money
in casinos. The player who judiciously applies the advice given
in this chapter will rarely find himself in a cheating situation.

11   DEALING WITH THE DEALER

Tipping the Dealer

Knowing when and how to tip the dealer can be critical to winning. Here is how to go about it. First of all, the general philosophy is to never give the dealer any money as a tip. Whenever you tip him place a bet for him. This is very common in the casinos. The proper procedure is for you to put a chip above your chips on the upper part of the betting spot. All dealers know exactly what this means. They know that this is a bet for them and they know that if you win your hand, they will pay you and will also pay off this extra chip that's sitting above your pile of chips. They know this is a bet for them. Thus, when you tip the dealer, always place a bet for him. The tip is always in the form of a bet.

There is a purpose to betting for the dealer. One very important reason for betting for the dealer is to tell him that you are on his side, that you are looking after him. If he is a cheating dealer this may make him think twice before he begins to cheat you. He will cheat you anyway if you are winning money or if the policy in that casino on that shift is for them to cheat players regularly. However, he may wait a few minutes before beginning to cheat you to show his appreciation for the fact that you have made a bet for him. If you are playing against an honest dealer it is also a good policy to make a bet for him because he may deal further down in the deck instead of shuffling up on you quickly. As soon as I win a big bet or as soon as I win several small bets I immediately place a bet for the dealer. The idea here is to make a bet for the dealer as quickly as you can after you start winning so that he will not begin to cheat you or shuffle up on you right from the beginning.

Another time for tipping the dealer is when you want him to deal further down in the deck than he usually deals. Most dealers deal to a certain level in the deck, usually three-quarters of the deck, or in some casinos such as Harrah's, they deal two-thirds of the deck. At any rate, each dealer deals down to a certain level of

the deck and then shuffles up. If you want the dealer to deal
another hand out then use the tip. When you have a high plus count
and you're down to about two-thirds of the deck, it is a very, very
good idea to place a bet for the dealer before the next round of
cards is dealt. Nine times out of ten the dealer will deal that
extra hand, especially when you are playing alone or with just one
other player and he has enough cards in the deck. Obviously, if
you haven't recognized it yet, this is out and out bribing the
dealer. But all is fair in love, war, and gambling.

Getting Personal With The Dealer

If you are using a simple point count and have learned it
to such a degree along with the strategy that you can engage in a
conversation while playing, it is a very good idea to get personal
with the dealer. That is, start asking how long he has been dealing,
where he has dealt before, where he is from. Tell a few stories
and crack a few jokes. This makes it very difficult for most
cheating dealers to concentrate. It helps if you can tell a few
jokes or funny stories. Then they really lose their concentration.
I was playing at the same table with a joker one time at Brutus'
Cave. At first, things were quiet. We were both losing and the
dealer was making hand after hand after hand. Then this guy started
to joke around. His jokes were so funny that one of the pit bosses
came over and started to laugh and tell stories himself. Everybody
was having a good time. Another player sat down at our table, we
all continued laughing and we all kept on winning from then on.
That was a very good experience. The thing not to do when you're
talking to the dealer is to complain. Never complain. These dealers
get complaints all the time. Complaints are the last thing he wants
to hear. It's very depressing. Try to cheer the dealer up without
being too obvious about it. The best way to cheer him up of course
is to make a bet for him. One thing I found that really works
with female dealers is the SMILE. It's very good to smile as you
walk up to the table where a girl is dealing. Just smile and keep on

smiling and make a few pleasant remarks. Most of them will smile
back and become cheerful and friendly towards you.

Hit and Run

Most dealers deal honestly when you first sit down to
play. I'm not sure why this is the case. Perhaps they are waiting,
wishing that you would win the first few hands so that you would
make a bet for them. Or perhaps they are dealing honestly to see how
good a player you are so that if you are a counter then they know
that they must cheat you. Whatever the case may be, I have found on
a lot of occasions that I begin to win money after 10 or 15 minutes
at the table, then things turn around and I begin to lose money, especially by losing big bets. The reason for this is that most dealers in
large casinos are cheating dealers to begin with and that most of
them are told not to let anybody win any appreciable amount of money.
I also know that the dealer's livelihood depends largely on the tips
that he gets from players. Now if a dealer is going to get tips
then he must allow the players to win a few hands at least. Nobody
makes a bet for the dealer if they are losing (unless they are crazy).
Thus a dealer may deal honestly at first, hoping that you will get up
a few units on him so that you will make a bet for him. Then later on
he knows that if he is to keep his job secure he must gradually or
very quickly take the money back that you have won. THIS IS WHEN TO RUN.
As soon as you lose two or three large bets quit right away.

Slow Down The Dealer

Many players I have taught privately complain that a lot of
dealers deal so fast that they can't concentrate on how to play and
they lose track of the count. As far as I have been able to determine there is no excuse for this. It is very easy to slow down the
dealer. All you have to do is not give him a signal until you are
perfectly sure how you want to play your hand. A lot of players are
intimidated by the dealer. The majority of dealers intimidate players

on purpose. Here is how they do it. If you should sit down alone
at the table and begin to play you'll notice that the dealer will
start dealing quite slowly. Then very, very gradually he will pick
up the pace of the deal. He will be dealing gradually faster and
faster, from shuffle to shuffle, from hand to hand. He wants to get
you into his rhythm of play. Since the dealer does this gradually,
most players do not become aware of what is happening. What they
do realize, though, after playing for 15 or 20 minutes is that they
feel rushed. Most players do not want to admit that they can't
play as fast as the dealer can deal, so they usually stand more
often, or don't get as big a bet out as quickly as they otherwise
would. Generally, they play an inferior brand of blackjack. Don't
let this happen to you. This is ridiculous. Right from the beginning, play at your pace and don't let the dealer get you into his
rhythm. The way to play at your pace is to be very slow and methodical and give very clear signals to the dealer. If you want a
hit, scratch your cards, if you don't want a hit have a look at your
cards first, look at them twice, then slowly put them under your
chips. Take your time and really slow down the dealer so that he
is playing your game instead of him intimidating you to play his
game. This can be done without effort after you have consciously
practised it two or three times. After this, it will become your
normal way of playing. Don't overdo it though. Don't be too slow
or you may irritate the dealer or any other players at your table.

Is He Hot?

This is a very good question to ask of players already
playing at a table at which you are about to sit down. As you are
walking up to the table simply smile and ask the first player that
turns around, "How's he been, is he hot?" If the player says, "Yeah
he's hot. He keeps on getting blackjacks", don't bother sitting
down at the table. Just walk out of the casino. You do not need to
ask this question very often, only when you are not sure whether the
players have been winning or losing at that table. It is easy to tell

if the players have been winning at the table. If they all have
a lot of chips in front of them they have been winning. If they
don't have a lot of chips in front of them it's hard to tell whether
they have been winning or losing. So this is a good time to
ask the question whether the dealer is hot or cold. Sometimes you
don't even have to ask the question. You can hear from a table
or two away players complaining about how hot the dealer is and
that he never busts. You hear ooohs when the dealer keeps making
good hands. The best example I've ever encountered of this was one
day about 10:30 in the morning. I was walking between the tables
at the Sea Inn on the Strip. I started to walk up to a table where
there was just one player playing, a gentleman in his fities. He
started to get up as I approached the table and said to the dealer,
"You know Lou, I've been coming here every Sunday morning for seven
years and I haven't beat you yet!" That was enough for me. I just
kept on walking.

Reading The Dealer

          After you have become an expert player, you can add a new
dimension to your game. This dimension is called reading the dealer.
It is a skill that many card players, not just blackjack players
learn very early in their card-playing days. By reading the dealer
what is meant is looking for tell-tale signs which give away the
dealer's hole card. Recently this has been labelled body-language.
Here are a few examples. Some of the inexperienced dealers, when
they have a ten-value card up, will look clumsily underneath to see
if they have an ace. Because of their inexperience a lot of times
they look so quickly they don't remember what the card underneath was
Or they don't see enough of it. So they have to look again. Now
when they do this it is a pretty good sign that the card underneath
was not a face card but rather that it was a smaller card. It's very
easy to see a face card. You don't have to see very much of a face
card in order to know that it is a face card. Face cards have a lot
of paint. But it's difficult to know whether a small card such as

48

a two, four or seven is an ace. Conversely, very rarely will an inexperienced dealer look underneath his up card twice if he has a ten-value card underneath. When the dealer does look under there twice chances are more likely than not that he has a small card under there. Since he has a ten-value card on top, then the thing to do is to stand if you have any kind of a stiff, that is any hand of twelve to sixteen. He has a good chance to bust now. If you have a soft hand, the thing to do would be to double in this situation. Also of course, if you have a nine, ten, or eleven, the thing to do would be to double in this situation, especially when the count is on the plus side. This alternate form of playing adds a great amount to your advantage.

Here is another way in which some dealers give themselves away. When they have a ten-value card on top and they've looked underneath, if they have a card underneath that makes up a good hand some dealers will place their fingers somewhere away from their up card. That is, when they have a solid hand they don't have to draw to they leave the hand alone. But when they know that they have to hit (when they have a small card under there) they usually place their fingers close to the up card so that when they turn the cards over they are ready to hit. Of course, when you can read a dealer in this way and know what his total hand is you have a great advantage. If he has a stiff you double your bet (if you can) or split pairs even though you would not play this way normally. If you read his hand as a good hand then you can surrender and save half of your bet (if that casino allows you to surrender).

The many different methods of dealing with the dealer will help you win money at a faster rate than you normally do. Other ways of handling the dealer are sprinkled throughout the book under more appropriate headings.

12   PLAYING CONDITIONS IN SPECIFIC CASINOS

International Blackjack Club members were surveyed and asked
how many times they won and lost in each casino they played in.
Each playing session was one hour long on the average. Table P shows
how well players did in specific casinos. Table P shows the total
number of times players played in each casino, the number of times
they won and the number of times they lost. The per cent of times
the players won is also given; this was simply calculated by taking
the number of times won over the total number of times played. The
higher this percentage the safer is the casino to play in. The
last column in Table P gives a ranking of all the casinos starting
with a rank of (1) for the safest casino and ending with a rank of
(39) for the least safe casino. It is seen that the 10 safest
casinos are, in order, Jackpot, Paradise Island, Sahara in Lake
Tahoe, Silver Slipper, Circus Circus, Paradise Casino, Royal Inn,
Aladdin, Horseshoe, and the casinos in Aruba. It is extremely
interesting that only two of the big Las Vegas Strip casinos made
the top ten. The moral here is to stay away from the Strip.

The least safe casinos, in order from the worst up, are
Harold's, Harrah's in Lake Tahoe, Marina, Frontier, Caesar's
Palace, Golden Gate, Tropicana, Castaways, Dunes, Riviera. It is
very instructive that out of the 10 worst casinos, 7 of them are
on the Strip. The moral again is to stay off the Strip.

The evidence presented is scientifically sound. It is
fact, not opinion. The players who were surveyed did not know one
another. There was no possibility of collusion. Such surveys are
carried out regularly by the International Blackjack Club. The
membership fee is $15 annually. See the centerfold for further
information.

TABLE P: PLAYING CONDITIONS IN SPECIFIC CASINOS

Table P shows (1) the total number of times players played in
different casinos, (2) the number of times they WON, (3) the number
of times they LOST, and as a summary statistic (4) the number of
times they WON is converted to the PER CENT of times they WON.
In column (5) the casinos are ranked from BEST which got a rank of
1 to worst which got a rank of 39.   The ranks are based on the percentages given in column (4).

	Total	Won	Lost	% Won	Rank		Total	Won	Lost	% Won	Rank
Aladdin	46	30	16	65.2	(8)	Horseshoe	171	111	60	64.9	(9)
Aruba	22	14	8	63.6	(10)	Jackpot	22	19	3	86.3	(1)
Caesar's Palace	293	131	162	44.7	(35)	Landmark	64	39	25	60.9	(19)
Castaways	26	13	13	50.0	(32)	Marina	19	8	11	42.1	(37)
Circus Circus	132	95	37	71.9	(5)	MGM Grand	404	224	180	55.4	(28)
Desert Inn	160	99	61	61.8	(16)	Mint	24	50	29	63.3	(11)
Dunes	295	149	146	50.5	(31)	Paradise Casino	93	63	30	67.7	(6)
El Cortez	34	21	13	61.7	(17)	Paradise Island	14	11	3	78.5	(2)
Flamingo	57	33	24	57.9	(24)	Riviera	175	89	86	50.8	(30)
Fremont	110	61	49	55.4	(29)	Royal Inn	36	24	12	66.6	(7)
Four Queens	74	46	28	62.2	(13)	Royal Las Vegas	28	16	12	57.1	(25)
Frontier	108	46	62	42.6	(36)	Sahara	196	124	72	63.2	(12)
Golden Gate	24	11	13	45.8	(34)	Sahara (Lake Tahoe)	26	20	6	76.9	(3)
Golden Nugget	68	40	28	58.8	(23)	Sands	151	92	59	60.9	(20)
Hacienda	48	27	21	56.2	(27)	Silver Slipper	37	27	10	72.9	(4)
Harold's	17	1	16	05.9	(39)	Stardust	83	51	32	61.4	(18)
Harrah's (Lake Tahoe)	35	11	24	31.4	(38)	Thunderbird	62	35	27	56.4	(26)
Harvey's (Lake Tahoe)	29	18	11	62.1	(15)	Tropicana	70	34	36	48.5	(33)
Hilton	182	113	69	62.1	(14)	Union Plaza	38	23	15	60.5	(22)
Holiday Inn	56	34	22	60.7	(21)						

THE CENTERFOLD

    The Centerfold has been moved to the Appendix. Excuse us
for this inconvenience but we did not want you to risk ruining your
book by having to tear out sheets from its center.

    The Appendix contains information on the HI-OPT, the HI-OPT II,
the International Blackjack Club, and how to order extra copies of
Blackjack Gold.

13   ADVANTAGES OF HEAD-ON PLAY

The best time to play is when the tables are not crowded.
The ideal situation is to play alone at the table. Playing
"head-on" with the dealer has many advantages. When you play
head-on you get to play more hands per hour than when there
are other players at your table. And the more hands you play per
unit of time the more money you turn over. The more money you
turn over the more money you will win, assuming you are playing
with a winning strategy.

The second advantage of playing head-on is that you get
to see all of the cards. When playing with others at the table
you often miss seeing some of the cards in the other player's
hands. It is important to see every card if you are to gain a good
advantage on the house. If you do not see some cards then your
count will be inaccurate. With an inaccurate count you will be
playing and betting inaccurately. Such play takes away from your
advantage.

The third advantage of head-on play is the conservation of
mental energy. The more players at your table the more mental
effort is required to watch and count all the cards. With a full
table of seven players it requires seven times the energy, to keep
track of cards than it does with only one player (you) at the table.
This is not the whole sad story. What is more unfortunate is that
the law of diminishing returns begins to operate with every
additional player that sits at your table. That is, the more
players at your table the more effort it takes you to win less
money, because you are getting fewer hands per hour.

A fourth advantage of head-on play is that more hands are
dealt between shuffles. This is good for the player because
shuffling is a waste of time (you can't play while the cards are
being shuffled). More importantly, with fewer shuffles, higher
count values result. Higher count values afford the player the
opportunity to make more money by placing larger wagers more often.

Other advantages of head-on play relate to not getting bothered by other players. Other players can bother you in many different ways. They can distract you innocently by asking you if the seat beside you is free. They can be more of a nuisance when they attempt to start a conversation with you. They can also alienate your dealer by complaining or not tipping him when they win. If the dealer is a cheat, he will take out his anger on the whole table, which includes you. (Cheating dealers do not discriminate at a full table because the easiest way for them to cheat is to deal themselves winning hands, like twenties or blackjacks).

If you're a non-smoker, a smoker joining your table can quickly kill your concentration. Unfortunately, most blackjack players smoke. They smoke more while playing too, due to the tension created by the game and the fact that the cigarettes are free.

If the other players at your table are poor players, their poor play can be very taxing on your self-control. Although you should know (as a professional) that the manner in which another player plays his hand has absolutely no effect on your hand (in the long run) it can be quite upsetting when someone takes the ten you needed on your eleven double-down hand by drawing vs. a six with a hand of fourteen. This actually happened to me at the Riviera when I had $400 on the table after doubling down with a $200 hand. Needless to say, I lost the $400. No matter how tough a player you are it is difficult to maintain one's composure in such situations. It is better to avoid them.

Another disadvantage of playing with others is the fact that they increase the probability that the pit boss will come over to the table. A pit boss at your table is not good for your playing longevity. Not only will he be able to watch your betting but he may even ask you your name and where you are from.

Another drawback of a crowded table is the fact that you have very little, if any, control over the game. You cannot speed the game up or slow it down when there are others at your table. You

don't get to cut the deck very often either. Neither can you
control the dealer by betting for him as you can in head-on
play. See the section on DEALING WITH THE DEALER for more details.

Disadvantages of head-on play

There is only one disadvantage to head-on play. It has
nothing to do with the dealer. The disadvantage is that the pit
boss or the eye-in-the-sky can watch you more easily since you
are the only one at the table. This problem is avoided by not
playing for more than 30 minutes in any one casino.

When can I find a head-on game?

The best time to find a dealer alone is on the graveyard
shift. This shift is on from midnight to eight o'clock in the
morning. On weekdays, the tables are very quiet between 3 a.m. and
10 a.m. On weekends you have to wait until after 4 a.m. to play
on this shift. It is getting more difficult to find good conditions
on this shift. This is because the casino likes to close most of
the tables down after the midnight show crowd leaves the casino.
In this way they force players to crowd together on the few tables
that remain open.
Another problem with playing on the graveyard shift is that
the casino is used to finding counters playing at that time. The
dealers tend to watch for counters more on this shift. However, the
optimum time to play on this shift is after 5 a.m. This is when the
dealers are tired. They have already worked five hours and are
looking forward to going home. They are physically weak (especially
on weekeneds because of the crowded tables till 4 a.m.) and mentally
lazy at this time. They deal slowly and usually don't take the extra
effort to cheat you at this time.
Other good times to play are during show times when most

people are watching the show. This can be from about 8 p.m. to
9:30 p.m. and from midnight to 1:30 a.m.

Another good time to play is when a new shift comes on.
The best time in this case in 12 noon. It is at noon that most
casinos open most of their tables for play. You can play for
about 30 minutes at this time before the tables become crowded.

Although there are no other specific times at which playing
conditions are best there is one important method of locating good
conditions. I have found that some casinos are very uncrowded at
exactly the same time a casino close by is jammed. When the MGM
Grand or the Dunes are crowded, for example, the Flamingo is
usually dead. When the Riviera and Circus Circus are jumping,
the Stardust or the Frontier are quiet. When the Sahara is full
the Hilton or Landmark can be good places for a head-on game. Therefore, as soon as the casino you are in becomes crowded try the place
next door.

In general, it is best to avoid playing on weekends. Las
Vegas, Reno, and Lake Tahoe casinos are overcrowded on weekends.
The only places you can find ideal conditions on weekends are on the
outskirts of town.

In terms of the seasons of the year, the winter months are
much better than the summer months. Tourists swarm all the casinos
during the summer. The deadest three weeks of the year are the first
three weeks in December. The playing conditions during these few
weeks are absolutely perfect.

No matter how bad the conditions, don't quit if you're winning

If you are a compulsive perfectionist, ignore this paragraph.
If you are normal, serious player whose chief aim is to win money
playing blackjack then this piece of advice will help you. The
advice is NEVER QUIT PLAYING IF YOU ARE WINNING, NO MATTER HOW BAD
THE CONDITIONS. If you are winning and the table becomes crowded
DON'T QUIT, KEEP PLAYING. If a drunk sits besides you and starts

swearing, put up with him IF YOU ARE WINNING. If the dealer
begins to hide cards on you and you lose the count KEEP PLAYING
IF YOU ARE WINNING. Do you get the idea? The name of the game
is to win money. Take the money under any and all conditions.
However, as soon as you start to lose, RUN no matter how good
the conditions. I like to quit after losing three or four large
bets in a row. You may want to set a different STOP-LOSS LIMIT
for yourself. Whatever you make your LOSS LIMIT, stick to it or
you will wind up a loser.

A friend of mine, let's call him Ron, has a stop-loss limit
of $2,000. Ron plays blackjack for a living, usually earning in
excess of $50,000 each year. Although he is a professional he
is not perfect. Sometimes he continues to gamble after being down
$2,000. According to his records, Ron found that he would be up
$34,000 more than he now is if he had always stuck to his $2,000
stop-loss limit. (This was over a period of three years).

The lesson is this. Always set a loss-limit for yourself.
If you don't you will never win any big money. If you do set a
loss-limit, you will never lose any big money.

An ancient philosopher named Tao said:

When the superior man gets his opportunity he
mounts aloft; but when the time is against him, he
is carried along by the force of circumstances.

By all means, "mount aloft" when you are winning. But do
not allow yourself to be "carried along by the force of circumstances".
QUIT instead. Oswald Jacoby, a gambling expert, has produced a
diagram to give you a better picture of when to quit. The diagram
is on the next page. If you memorize it and use it you will rarely
lose very much money while gambling.

THE QUITTING CURVE

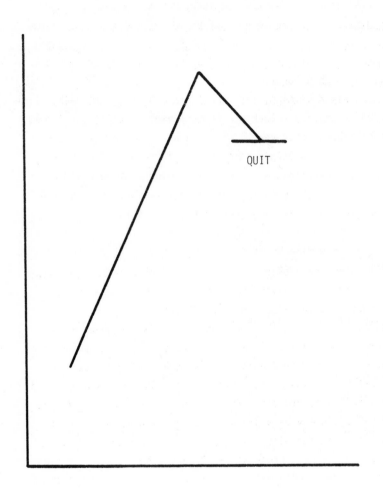

QUIT

14   METHODS OF WAGERING (MONEY MANAGEMENT)

There is no single best way to bet in blackjack. In
general, the safest and, at the same time, most profitable long-
term method of wagering is to bet more money the greater your
advantage. The size of your count should be taken as an indication
of the advantage you have at any particular time. The greater the
plus count the greater the advantage. The greater the negative count
the greater the disadvantage. Whenever your count is zero or negative (minus) bet the minimum bet, one unit, because the house has
the advantage(usually). Whenever the count is plus one (+1) or
higher bet more than one unit because you have the advantage. The
greater the plus count the more hands you will win and the fewer
hands the dealer will win. Obviously, when you know you are going
to win more hands than the dealer you should bet more money.

The Kelly Criterion and the True Count
        According to Professor J. L. Kelly the perfect betting method
is to bet a percentage of your total bankroll that corresponds to
the exact percentage advantage you have on your bet. For example,
if your total bankroll is 100 units and your advantage on the next
hand you are to be dealt is 2 per cent, you should bet 2 per cent of
100 units, which would be 2 units. This method is known as the
KELLY CRITERION. It was first published in 1956 and was applied to
blackjack wagering by Professor Thorp in his book Beat the Dealer.
The KELLY CRITERION may be applied to all gambling games (not just
blackjack) in which the player has an advantage and knows what it
is in percentage terms. Professor Kelly and other scientists have
proven both mathematically and in practice that the Kelly method is
the most profitable long-run method of wagering. It yields the
greatest profits with the smallest amount of risk, in the long term.

How do we apply the KELLY CRITERION to blackjack? Methods
of betting which approximate the KELLY CRITERION are very easy
to invent. For example, the simplest method is to bet the same
number of chips as your count: if your count is +2 bet 2 chips,
if the count is +4 bet 4 chips, etc. This is the safest and most
profitable way to bet when playing against a single deck. When
playing against more than a single deck, if we want to have the
same advantage as with a single deck, we should first divide our
running count by the number of decks we are playing against and
we should wager according to this new TRUE COUNT. Thus, against
two decks we divide our actual or running count by 2; against
four decks we divide it by 4; when there are only 3 decks left in
a 4-deck game we would divide our running count by 3. For example,
if we just started to play in a four deck game and the count
quickly reached +8, we would divide by 4 (since there are almost 4
decks left in the shoe) and get a TRUE COUNT of +2, indicating
a bet of 2 units.

The reason for the need to compute the TRUE COUNT is because
it has been mathematically shown that the casinos have a greater
advantage the more decks they use. The true count is the method
with which such greater advantages can be fairly accurately
equalized to the theoretical one deck level.

There are several betting methods shown in the figures below.
You may wager according to the true count as described above in
all of the methods (except in Method 1, flat betting, in which
there is no variation of bets). However, most players prefer to
wager according to the RUNNING COUNT. They do not bother dividing
by the number of decks. The reason they prefer the running count is
because it affords more betting opportunities. The opportunities
are not as safe, according to mathematical advantage, as the TRUE
COUNT opportunities but there are many more of them. It is precisely
because of this latter fact that I recommend wagering according to
the RUNNING COUNT. There are so many more opportunities to increase

the sizes of the wagers that the long-term profit becomes much greater than wagering according to the true count. However, because it is riskier to wager with the RUNNING COUNT than with the TRUE COUNT, a greater initial BANKROLL is needed.

The Bankroll

The size of the BANKROLL is extremely important. The BANKROLL must be large enough to sustain any unfavourable fluctuations in the game. Many players with winning blackjack systems fail to win because they overbet. The wagering must be systematic, methodical, conservative and always according to one's total bankroll. The recommended bankroll sizes will now be given.

TRUE COUNT wagering requires a BANKROLL of 50 times the size of the largest bet.

RUNNING COUNT wagering requires a BANKROLL 100 times the size of the largest bet (except in single deck play, 50 is adequate).

ANY PLUS COUNT wagering requires a BANKROLL 200 times the size of the largest bet (except in single deck play, 100 is adequate). By "any" count is meant raising your bet size at any plus count; thus, one may wager as much as 8 units on a RUNNING COUNT of only +1.

Here is an explication of the recommendations.

In Method 2 below, the largest wager is 2 units. TRUE COUNT wagering would require a BANKROLL of 2 x 50 = 100 units. RUNNING COUNT wagering requires 2 x 100 = 200 units. ANY PLUS COUNT wagering requires 2 x 200 = 400 units.

In Method 4 below, the largest wager is 8 units. TRUE COUNT wagering requires a BANKROLL of 8 x 50 = 400 units. RUNNING COUNT requires 8 x 100 = 800 units. ANY PLUS COUNT requires 8 x 200 = 1600 units.

Conclusion

The wagering advice given in this chapter is meant to protect the player from being ruined by wild fluctuations that so often occur

in blackjack. By following the advice the player will never be
ruined in terms of losing his entire bankroll (assuming an honest
game, of course). According to the wagering advice presented it is
impossible for a player to overbet if he follows the advice. The
player has a choice of five betting methods. He may choose which-
ever method suits his personal style and bankroll. The advanced
player may wish to experiment with modifications of any of the methods
given. The variations are almost infinite.

The important point to grasp is this. The player who adopts
the wagering advice and methods given here (assuming he can avoid
being cheated) will not only not lose his starting bankroll but
will start winning money and continue to win as long as he continues
playing. That is, he can never lose, he will only win. If he
wishes, the player can verify this fact for himself by playing in a
completely honest game at home with friends.

Methods of Wagering

Method 1: For single deck play only. Wager the same
amount every time. This is known as FLAT betting. You bet the same
amount of money all the time, no matter what the count is. This
is the most conservative method of betting possible. This method
can only be used with a powerful playing strategy such as the HI-OPT
or the HI-OPT II. Either of these strategies will produce close
to a 1% gain on flat bets. (The HI-OPT strategies are described
in the centerfold). Flat betting is the perfect method for players
who wish to avoid getting barred. The casinos have never barred
anyone who flat bet. This method is recommended for players betting
25 dollar units or greater amounts. Also, since the advantage
is relatively small (about 1%) a bankroll of 200 units (200 x $25 =
$5000) is recommended.

Method 2:   For single deck play only. Start either with one or two
units then follow the diagram below. (Our thanks to Dr. Koko Ita
for the idea of the diagrams). Method 2 is recommended for players
betting 20 dollar units or greater amounts. Method 2 is another
conservative betting method. It is extremely unlikely that one will
ever get barred using this method. However, in order for this method
to yield a worthwhile hourly profit it should be used with one of the
HI-OPT strategies. Or, alternatively, when using the BASIC strategy
the unit bet should be raised to $40.00. For bankroll requirements
for this and the other methods below follow the text.

Your first bet is one or two units:

If your last bet was | and if you | and the count is | your bet now is

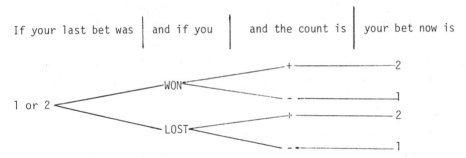

Method 3. For single or double deck play.

Your first bet is one unit:

If your last
bet was   and if you   and the count is   your bet now is

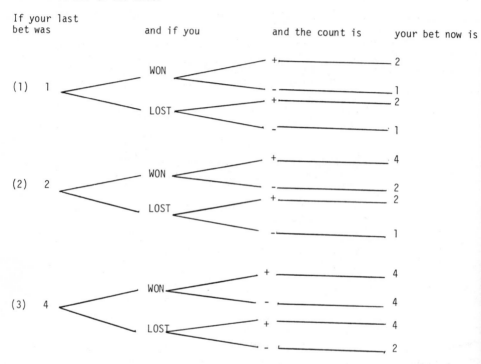

Method 3 is recommended for 5 and 25 dollar chip bettors.

Method 4. For single, double or multiple deck play.

Your first bet is 4 units. Follow steps (1) and (2) of method 3 unless:

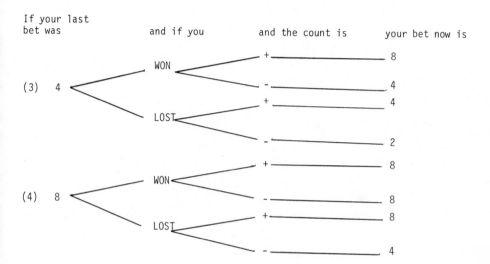

If your last
bet was   and if you   and the count is   your bet now is

Method 4 is recommended for 5 dollar unit chip bettors and for 2 dollar unit chip bettors.

NOTE: When using Method 4 against 4 or more decks, your first bet should be 2 (not 4) units. And the bet size should not be increased until the true count reaches +4.

Method 5. For four or six deck play. Your first bet is 2 units. Use Method 4 except: when you win an 8-unit bet place the 8 units you just won on a second hand if the count is plus four or more. Thus, we are recommending you play two hands in a multiple deck game with 8 units on each hand when you have a clear advantage.

To further protect yourself from getting barred we recommend this practice: do not alter the size of the bet you have
in front of you should the dealer catch you by surprise and shuffle
the deck on you. That is, do not touch your bet no matter how
large it may be. True, you are giving up an advantage in cases where
you are left with a large bet (two 8 unit bets, for example, in a
4-deck game) at the shuffle. But such sacrifices must be recognized
as being necessary for survival.

The Playing Bankroll
        There are two kinds of bankrolls. There is the total bankroll.
The total bankroll was discussed above under the heading "Bankroll".
The second kind of bankroll is the Playing Bankroll. The playing
bankroll is the amount of money you need for one playing session.
That is, you are not expected to carry around with you your total
bankroll. You only need several small amounts of money as playing
bankrolls for one day. The size of your playing bankroll should be
related to the particular method of betting which you employ. The
following is recommended.

Wagering Method	Bet Range	Playing Bankroll
1	Flat	8
2	1-2	10
3	1-4	16
4	1-8	32
5	1-16	64

        The playing bankrolls are in terms of units. For example,
Method 1 requires 8 units or bets, Method 5 requires 64 unit bets.
Do not lose more than one playing bankroll in any one playing session.
If you suspect the dealer quit even before losing your entire playing
bankroll.

When sitting down to buy chips buy as few as possible.
That is, buy only half or one-quarter of the number of units needed
for your entire playing bankroll. For example, if using Method 5
buy only 16 units worth of chips instead of the 64 required. You
can buy more later should you need to. The reason for this advice
is so that you never show the casino how much money you have.
The less money you appear to have the less of a threat you are in
their eyes.

15   HOW NOT TO GET BARRED

There are literally dozens of techniques one may use to camouflage one's play so as not to get barred. The exposition which follows is believed to be the most comprehensive ever written on this subject.

1) Don't play for more than 30 minutes in any one casino.

It is important that you don't play for more than a few minutes in any one casino. The reasons for this are obvious. The dealer and pit bosses are constantly on the look out for winning players. Winning players are either barred, shuffled up on, or cheated. The less time that you spend winning in any one casino, the longer will your playing life be. I know some players that when playing in a casino which has shoes will only play through one shoe and then they will leave the casino, win or lose. Other players when playing in casinos where they have single or double deck games, will quit as soon as they have won a few large wagers and then begin to lose. Some players quit after as little time as playing for five minutes in a casino. These players may come into a casino and watch a blackjack game in progress, wait until the count is positive, then place a large wager and keep playing while the count is positive, then leave when the dealer shuffles up the deck. If you are not worried about getting barred, then I recommend a different method of play. As is the case with me, I am easily recognized in most casinos in Las Vegas. Therefore, whenever I am allowed to play in a casino like any normal player in a casino, that is without being cheated or being shuffled up on, then I will stay in that casino and keep play- ing until I start to lose some large wagers. Sometimes I've played for over 2 hours, as long as I was winning. I stay and gradually in- crease the size of my bets and try to win as much money as possible at that one sitting in that casino. I strongly recommend that you play in the same way if you are not concerned with getting barred.

2) Don't jump your bets

The easiest way for you to give yourself away as a counter is to jump your bets while playing. The dealers and pit bosses have learned to watch erratic betting more than any other feature of blackjack play. By jumping your bets I mean betting one unit all along and then when the count becomes positive, betting three or more units. The recommended procedure of raising one's bet is to wait until the bet has won and then simply let the winnings ride on the next hand. This is called parlaying. The only exception to this kind of parlay betting is to jump your bets from one unit up to two units. This is the only kind of jump that the casino personnel will tolerate, since it is only a small jump. However, do not even make this small jump if you are the cautious type. Specific methods of wagering to disguise one's increases in bets are depicted in the figures on wagering methods in this volume.

3) Don't move your lips while counting

This may seem to be an obvious piece of advice. Nevertheless, have you ever watched yourself playing blackjack in a mirror? I have. It's amazing how serious one can appear when playing blackjack. And your lips actually do move unless you have practiced watching yourself count in a mirror and have trained yourself to keep your mouth closed while counting. If you keep your mouth closed your tongue will sometimes move but this is not possible to detect by anyone observing from the outside.

4) Don't move your head

Many counters give themselves away by moving their head while they are counting the cards as they are being dealt. This is something that is very common to amateur blackjack players. Again, practise in front of a mirror and watch yourself, or ask someone else to watch your head to see if it moves while you are following the cards. It is better to find a seat with a direct visual perspective on the table top to minimize head movements. The seat that I

have found to be ideal for this purpose is the second last seat at
the table. This is the seat which is near third base. It is the
seat that is on the dealer's right-hand side, next to the end seat.
Another important method for preventing your head from moving is
not to count the cards until they have all been dealt. That is,
don't follow the cards as they are coming out of the dealer's hand
and falling on the table. Wait until all the players' hands are
dealt, then count all the cards as you see them. This is the
preferred method of counting cards by most players. Not only does
this method prevent you from moving your head quickly back and
forth, it also makes it much easier to keep the count accurately.

5) When playing against the shoe, quit at the end of the shoe
    if your last bet was a large one.

        This is a rather detailed move. Some players I know actually
do quit when the dealer starts shuffling up the shoe and when the bet
that they have on the table is a large bet. This is because the
dealer will see you change your bet when he begins dealing out of
the freshly shuffled shoe. That is, the casino has the advantage
at the beginning of a fresh shoe so that the wisest bet is your
minimum bet at the beginning. If your last bet in the old shoe was
a large bet and your first bet in the new shoe is a small bet, it
will be quite obvious to the dealer and the pit boss that you are
probably keeping track of the cards. There is an alternative,
however, to quitting. And that is to leave your bet alone, even
if it was a large bet at the end of the shoe. This is a practice
that I recommend. True, you will be giving up a small advantage
by beginning play with a large wager against the shoe, however,
you will be able to continue playing in that particular casino
instead of wasting valuable playing time in running from casino to
casino.

6) Never leave the spot in front of you empty

        Never leave the rectangle in front of you empty when playing.

Be sure you always have a bet lying in the betting spot in front of you. You might wonder, "But how do I know how much to bet before I get the correct count?" You have to estimate what the probable count will be when the rest of the players have finished playing. That is, when you are playing with other players at the table, and there are players that have to play after you play, and you have just busted and lost your bet, you must immediately place another bet in the spot in front of you instead of waiting to see the other players' cards who have yet to play. True, this will take away slightly from your advantage when your estimate of the count turns out to be incorrect. However, it is better to have something up in that square, rather than giving yourself away to the dealer or pit boss. This piece of advice, of course, does not apply when you are alone playing head on against the dealer. The advantages of head on play are described in another part of this volume.

7) At the start of a new deal, don't always bet your minimum amount

This applies more to multiple than to single deck games. The casinos know that they have a built in advantage at the start of a multiple deck game. Most counters know this, therefore, most counters bet their minimum amount at the start of a multiple deck game. My advice is for you to sometimes bet two units instead of the minimum one unit at the beginning of such games, in order to throw the dealer off. Along with this advice, is the advice given in Point #5 above, which was not to touch your large bet if it was the last bet before the shuffle in a multiple deck game.

8) Don't hold up the game in any way

You must learn how to play smoothly. This can only come with practice. It is important because when you are alone at the table the dealer may be a fast dealer and if you try to slow him down on purpose he may get upset at you. An upset dealer can either shuffle up on you or cheat you. When you are playing with other players at the table, you must get into their rhythm of play so as not to disturb the atmosphere at the table. You can not draw

attention to yourself in any way. However, please don't mistake
this piece of advice and attempt to play beyond your capability.
If you are playing against a fast dealer and cannot keep the count,
you must slow him down. How to slow down the dealer is covered in
another part of this book.

9) Dress like the tourists

        It is important not to stand out in any way in terms of
dress from the other players. The weather is extremely hot in
Las Vegas for most of the year. Therefore, most people wear short-
sleeved shirts and women wear light blouses. On the Las Vegas Strip
the tourists are usually better dressed than the tourists in Downtown Las Vegas. Although the Strip tourists wear casual clothes
the casual clothes are usually flashier and more expensive than
the casuals that are worn by tourists in Downtown Las Vegas. If
you are gambling in Downtown Las Vegas you would look very much
like a tourist if you wore a short-sleeved checkered cowboy type of
a shirt and levis or plain, dull slacks. If you are playing Downtown
and want to stand out like a sore thumb then wear a sports jacket.
You can also wear expensive jewellry Downtown if you want to stand
out. Whenever I play downtown, I always wear a Timex watch and I
take the Cross pen out of my shirt pocket and put it in my pant
pocket where they can't see it. Dealers and pit bosses are very
alert when it comes to players' apparel, including jewellry. Most
players don't carry a pen in their shirt pocket at all. If you
do carry a pen there, then the dealer can very quickly infer that
you are some kind of a system player. In Las Vegas, they don't like
people with pens or pencils or pads. They don't like people to
keep track of their winnings or their losses. They just want people
to gamble without being aware of how much they are losing.

10) Don't allow the casino to choose your dealer for you

It has been my experience that the safest dealers to play against are young, female dealers. This fact has been confirmed by hundreds of players who belong to the International Blackjack Club. Club members were surveyed and asked how well they did playing against different kinds of dealers, young, old, male and female. Young female dealers turned out to be the safest to play against and older male and female dealers turned out to be the worst to play against. These results are shown in the table on the next page titled Table D: Dealers Information.

TABLE D: DEALERS INFORMATION

International Blackjack Club members were asked the following
question:

"What sex and age dealers have you had the best luck with in winning?"

Please rank them from best (1) to worst (5):

	August, 1975	April, 1976
Young girl dealers (under age 30)	1.80	1.86
Young boy dealers (under age 30)	2.64	1.93
Middle-aged women (30 to 45)	3.36	3.13
Middgle-aged men (30 to 45)	3.56	3.53
Older men and women (over 45)	3.60	3.86

It is obvious from Table D that young girl dealers are the best to play
against, young boy dealers the next best and all older dealers (over
30) the worst. This has also been my personal experience. A statistical
test was applied to the results of Table D and indicated significant
differences between the two youngest types of dealers and the three oldest.
The difference between the young girl dealers and the young boy dealers
was also statistically significant. In conclusion, the lesson to be
learned here is that the safest dealers to play against are young girl
dealers. And the dealers to avoid are all those over 30 years of age.
The statistical significance of the results suggests that they were
definitely not obtained by chance. The results of Table D are very
reliable because the same results were obtained from two different groups
of gamblers in two different surveys, one in August, 1975 and the other
in April, 1976. That is, older dealers must be doing something that the
younger ones are not doing!

Therefore, before sitting down to play in a casino you should
first walk around to see if you can spot any young female dealers.
If you can, then sit down and begin playing. Should you be winning
money after a few minutes you will often find that another dealer
comes to your table. This dealer is often older than the dealer
you chose. I advise you to quit playing immediately and cash out
your chips and leave the casino. If you don't quit at this time,
then you have just allowed the casino to choose your dealer for you.
It is standard practice for a casino to put tough dealers onto
players who have been winning in the casino. Therefore, don't let
the casino choose your dealer for you. Should the second dealer
be either a young girl dealer, or a young boy dealer, you can stay
and keep playing against the new dealer. However, should you start
losing, quit.

11) Don't be the biggest bettor at your table

If you play in downtown Las Vegas or other smaller casinos,
you will find that most players are betting dollar chips or $2.00
units. Some players will be betting $5.00 chips. Don't be the
only one at a $1.00 table who is betting $5.00 chips. Or don't
be the only one at a $5.00 table who is betting $25.00 chips. You
will be the only one that the dealer and the pit boss will be
watching. Pit bosses are instructed to always watch the biggest
bettor at each table.

12) Don't attract attention in any way

A number of good blackjack players attract attention by the
way they handle their cards. Since there are a lot of players who
cheat at blackjack, the dealers are instructed to watch any unusual
moves on the part of the players. Some players mark cards with
special paint which they get from underneath their fingernails.
Other cheaters bend cards or crimp them or mark them by cutting
them with their finger nails. Players have even been caught trying
to switch decks and bring in new cards into the game. Therefore,

be mindful of the way in which you hold your cards and always have
clean fingernails.

13) Tip the dealer

I make it a practice to place a wager for the dealer (this
is his tip) as soon as I am up a few hands. I want to let the
dealer know as soon as I am winning that I am looking after him.
This is extremely important when playing in Las Vegas in games
that are dealt out of the hands (this is not as critical in the shoe
game). Tipping the dealer by placing a wager for him in front of
your wager is a protection against being shuffled up on and against
being cheated. Don't get me wrong. They will still cheat you if
you are winning money. However, they will delay the process of
cheating you if you are betting for them. The thing to do then is
to bet for them as quickly as possible, but only if you are winning
money. Then when they start to cheat you, quit playing before you are
cheated out of all of your winnings. Also, only place the wager for
the dealer when the count is positive. This is obvious. When the
count is positive you have a better chance of winning the wager and
the dealer has a better chance of winning his tip.

14) Don't vary the size of your wager when a pit boss is watching

A few serious players that I know resort to flat betting
when the pit boss is watching. That is, whatever bet they had on
the table before the pit boss began watching them is the bet they
continue with until the pit boss goes away. Similarly, these players
don't vary their play from the basic strategy when a pit boss is
watching. (That is, if they are using one of the advanced strategies
such as the HI-OPT or the HI-OPT II, they cease using it and resort
to the basic strategy).

15) Never talk at the table

It is very important not to talk when playing. This is so
for several reasons. The most important reason not to talk is

so that you don't give your identity away to the dealer or pit boss.
Dealers can often tell where a person is from by their accent. I
have often been identified as a Canadian from the way I talk in Las
Vegas. Also, once you begin talking then other players tend to
talk more. This can obviously disturb your concentration. What is
worse, however, is that the pit boss is more likely to come over
to your table and ask your name and where you're from, and so on.
Pit bosses are instructed to get players' names, especially the
players who are betting large amounts of money. When they do get
your name, they phone the Central Credit Agency to check you out.
Central Credit has all the credit information on you. That is, if
you've ever been on a junket, how much money you los‌t, how you paid,
whether by cheque or cash, where you played, and so on and so on.
Therefore, if you want to protect your anonymity and prolong your
playing life, don't talk at the table. If you must talk then be
brief and polite.

16) <u>Smile!</u>

Don't look glum or serious while playing, you may alert
the house. Smile! I am not the smiling type. I had to practice
in front of a mirror in order to learn how to smile at a blackjack
table. Perhaps you may want to do the same. Try to be happy at the
table. If you must talk, don't complain. The dealers are sick of
hearing players complain. Complaints are the last thing the
dealer wants to hear. Now don't take this piece of advice literally.
If the dealer fails to pay you, please draw attention to that fact.
But don't complain unnecessarily.

17) <u>Drink while you play</u>

Drink while you play, but only if you can hold your liquor.
Casinos love drunks. As you know they provide players with free
drinks while they're playing. In fact, the drinks that they serve
to players are often stronger than the drinks they serve at the bar
to people who aren't playing. If you are a person that can drink
well, then by all means drink at the table. You will draw

suspicion away from yourself. Unfortunately, I do not drink.
When I do order something to drink, it's usually a Diet Pepsi.
The dealers and pit bosses always get a big laugh out of this.
If you are a non-drinker, then a good drink to order which is
completely non-alcoholic is an Orange Julius. This is a very tasty
and healthy drink which is something like a milkshake. The only
trouble I've found with ordering this drink is that after you
get it, it looks so appetizing that players at your table will
ask you what it is.

18) Don't tell the dealer or pit boss your name

This point was alluded to above. The dealer and more often
the pit boss are always trying to find out big bettors names. Big
bettors that I know use several different names when they are gambling.
In fact, there was a saying around Las Vegas that nobody gives their
right name in Las Vegas.

19) Play with a female companion (if you are a male)

A very good way to draw suspicion away from yourself as a
winning player is to play with a girl. Of course, you should teach
her the basic strategy first so that she doesn't lose any of your
money. The pit bosses love couples. They automatically assume that
the man can't play well and that he's not serious about winning money
because he's got his wife or girl friend with him. I know one
professional player who not only taught his female travelling com-
panion the basic strategy but also has worked out a series of signals
for her as to when she should raise the size of her wagers. His
very clever maneuver is to have her betting $200.00 when the count
is high-plus, where he is only betting $50.00 at the same time. Now
during the high positive counts, it's quite easy for the dealer to
realize that most of the tens and aces are still in the deck.When he
sees the man betting a small bet and the woman betting a big bet he
really becomes confused and assumes that the man doesn't know what
he's doing. After all, why should he trust a dumb broad with all that
money? This is the mentality of blackjack personnel when it comes

to females.

20) Don't be stubborn

Don't be stubborn and refuse to leave the table a loser.
The reason that most blackjack players, no matter how good they
are, lose money is because they refuse to quit while they're losing.
It is imperative that you set a STOP-LOSS limit for yourself when you
are playing blackjack. While you're playing, as soon as you hit
the amount of money that is your stop-loss limit, that is the
largest amount of money that you are willing to lose at one sitting,
quit.

The twenty points just listed should give you an idea of
how to behave at a blackjack table so as not to get barred. There
are a number of other pieces of advice about not getting barred
which are sprinkled throughout the book. Although some of the
points mentioned above may be obvious or even humorous, please try
to take them seriously. They are all very important for winning
money in casinos.

16   A THEORY OF PROFESSIONAL BLACKJACK

The theory of professional blackjack will be given in the form of nine requirements that are necessary for winning. These nine requirements were developed over several years. The requirements arose out of my experience in playing blackjack in the thirty trips which I made to Las Vegas in the early and middle 70's. I have come to the conclusion that there are nine things which are necessary if one is to play blackjack professionally. The nine requirements are listed below and then each requirement is taken and discussed separately.

1) A complete knowledge of the game.
2) The keeping of records.
3) Self-knowledge.
4) Independence of thought and confidence.
5) Mental readiness or total concentration.
6) Physical readiness.
7) A basic knowledge of probability theory.
8) Self-control.
9) A game plan.

1) A complete knowledge of the game

This is an obvious requirement. If one is to gamble professionally one needs to know everything there is to know about the game of blackjack. This includes not only knowing the basic strategy but also knowing a count system, knowing how to wager properly, and knowing how to protect oneself from being cheated. All these subjects are covered in the book. A complete knowledge of the game cannot be obtained from only reading this book. You are referred to the recommended books and publications at the end of the volume if you want to increase your knowledge of the game. Finally, there is no better teacher

than experience. Therefore, get as much casino playing experience
as possible, using small stakes at first while you are learning.
Even before venturing into a casino, however, you should have practised for many, many hours at home in order to prove to yourself
that you have mastered the rudiments of the game.

2) The keeping of records

It is critical to keep records in the game of blackjack.
One method of keeping records is shown on the next page. It is a
Playing Record Sheet. You may use the back of a blank cheque to make
such a sheet up. It is very convenient to use a cheque and carry it
in your wallet, rather than carrying a booklet around with you. If
examine the playing record sheet on the next page, you will see that
there are several headings. There is the date on which you are
playing. Next, there is the exact time of day when you are playing.
Next to that is recorded the name of the casino in which you are
playing. Then the next very important column is for the amount you
woi or lost in each playing session. Finally, there is a very wide
column for you to put down any comments you have about the dealer,
the pit boss, and the casino playing conditions in that specific
casino. This last column, the Dealer and Pit Boss Comments column
needs elaboration. In this column I record the dealer's name, if
he happens to be wearing a name-tag. I also record a description of
him or her. Most importantly, I record my impression as to whether
the dealer was honest or a cheat. Also in this column, I record to
what degree the pit boss was watching my play and whether he was
counting the cards along with me or not.
It is very important to keep such a record sheet, for many
reasons. For example, recording the time is important in case there
is a dealer or pit boss working at that time that knows you are a
winning player. The fact that you have recorded comments about the
dealer and pit boss will allow you to avoid playing in that particular casino at that particular time that the enemy dealer and pit
boss is working.

THE PLAYING RECORD SHEET

DATE	TIME	CASINO	WON/LOST	DEALER AND PIT BOSS COMMENTS

3) Self-knowledge

This is a psychological requirement. What it means is that
you must know yourself as a gambler. The activity of gambling is
so powerful that it can transform a person's personality totally.
Therefore, you must pay attention to your feelings, your thoughts and
your betting behaviours while you are gambling in order to learn
about yourself as a gambler. This is important so that you can know
whether to keep on gambling when for example, you are losing a lot
of money, or whether you should quit. It is also important to know
what your personality is like when you are gambling in relation to
how you behave with other players, or whether you can keep your cool
when playing against a dealer you do not like. Unfortunately, the
only way to learn about yourself as a gambler is by a lot of playing
experience.

4) Independence of thought and confidence

Pittsburgh Phil, the legendary millionaire horse-player, said
"A man who has not an opinion of his own, has not one chance in a
million to make money wagering on the thoroughbred". The same statement applies to all forms of gambling. If you are to gamble professionally, you must think for yourself. You must have confidence in
your own judgement and you must act independently. You cannot be
allowed to be influenced by other people, either friends or enemies.

5) Mental readiness or total concentration

This is another psychological requirement that is acquired
with playing experience. Mental readiness refers to being alert. This
is the ability to be able to concentrate on the cards regardless of
what is going on around you. You must develop the skill of concentration to such a degree that you can keep track of the cards and carry
on a conversation with the dealer or one of the players at the same time.
This is not as difficult to do as it may seem, specially if you are using
a simple point count such as the HI-OPT COUNT.

6) Physical readiness

Physical readiness refers to having your body ready to put
up with the strain that's involved in playing at least four hours
a day. By physical readiness I mean not only being in good physical
condition but also having an adequate amount of sleep. If you have
ever been to Las Vegas you will know that it is very difficult to
sleep there. Las Vegas is located in the middle of the desert, the
climate is very hot and very dry. Everything is open around the
clock, and the whole atmosphere is one of fantasy. It is very
difficult to keep one's biological balance in such an atmosphere.
The rule which I follow to keep physically ready when in Las Vegas
is the following: I pay attention to my body. When my body tells
me that it is tired, I go to sleep right away, no matter what time
of night or day it is. And I sleep until I am fully rested. That
is, I let my body dictate my playing hours and my sleeping hours.
I do not gamble when I am tired either mentally or physically.

7) A basic knowledge of probability theory

A knowledge of probability theory is needed for several
reasons. First, if you are familiar with probability theory you will
know what kinds of winning and losing streaks to expect in the game.
When you know what kinds of losing streaks to expect in the game,
you are less likely to accuse the dealer of cheating. That is, you
will not be as suspicious as often. It is not good for your mental
state to be suspicious. The second importance of probability theory
is related to the bankroll. The bankroll requirements are discussed
at length in this book. Briefly, you have to know the size of your
bankroll in relation to the percentage advantage you have with your
particular winning strategy. This is so that you do not lose a
possibly inadequate bankroll due to wild fluctuations in the game.

8) Self-Control

      This is by far the most important psychological requirement
in professional gambling. No matter how strong a strategy you
have, no matter how brilliant you may be, no matter how good your
photographic memory is, you will never win without self-control.
Self-control means controlling yourself when you are losing. You
must not be stubborn. When you begin to lose, quit. Quitting is
discussed in another part of the book.

9) A game plan
      The final requirement of a game plan, is a general, overall
requirement. This requirement brings in your philosophy or your
reason for playing the game of blackjack. That is, you must have it
very clear in your mind why you are devoting all these hours to the
game. Are you certain that you are spending all this time because
you want to win money at the game. Or are you spending all the time
because it is fun to play the game. If you are playing the game more
for fun than profit, then you don't have to be as concerned with winning.
However, if you are playing cold-bloodedly to win, you must have an
overall game plan. By an overall game plan I mean such things as
how many trips should I make to Las Vegas, how many days should I stay
there when I'm there, how big of a bankroll should I bring with me,
how many hours a day should I play, when should I quit, should I
socialize with people when I'm here or should I make it strictly a
business trip everytime. All these sorts of questions must be answered
when you are devising a game plan.

      There you have my theory of the professional gambler. You may
not agree with it. It is only one man's theory. Nevertheless, the
theory helps me tremendously when I use it. My performance sky-rockets.
I hope you make the effort to apply it to yourself.

17   THE PYSCHOLOGY OF GAMBLING

The science of psychology tries to explain why people
behave as they do. The psychology of gambling is the science
of explaining why people gamble. Most people do not gamble for
the purpose of winning money. Gambling experts such as Oswald
Jacoby estimate that less than one person in a hundred wins money
from gambling in the long run. The paradox is that although most
people lose money when gambling they continue to return to gamble
over and over again. The logical conclusion is that they are
gambling for psychological rather than monetary reasons. Thus
the psychology of gambling has to be consulted if we are to explain
the motivation to gamble.

Professor Igor Kusyszyn of the Psychology Department of
York University in Toronto, Canada is regarded as an academic
authority on the psychology of gambling. Dr. Kusyszyn and his
students have done a number of research studies with gamblers in
the last few years. The research findings suggest that people gamble
in order to satisfy two very basic human needs. These needs are:
1) the need to confirm one's existence; and 2) the need to affirm
one's worth. In order to understand the satisfaction of these two
basic needs, gambling must first be looked at as adult play. That
is gamblers gamble in order to play and not in order to win money.
They hope to win money but what they are really enjoying the most is
the action involved in gambling. That gambling is in fact play is
blatantly obvious when one examines the language surrounding gambling:
gamblers are referred to as players, be they card players, horse
players or bingo players; gamblers play games, they play cards and
they play horses; a wager on a horse race is called a play and so on.
Gamblers play with money rather than for money.

How does the gambler confirm his existence? The gambler confirms
his existence by getting aroused. The activity of gambling tends to
arouse a person mentally, emotionally, and physically. For example,
the gambler can increase his muscle tension or speed up his heart rate.

He can become emotionally aroused both positively with hope, excitement and euphoria, and negatively with anxiety, disappointment, frustration, sorrow and regret. Gambling also yields an opportunity for the experiencing of anger, hostility, and aggression, and for externalizing such negative states onto wives, husbands, onto the dealer, onto other players, onto pit bosses, and even onto the President and the Government. Descartes, the philosopher, said: "I think, therefore I am". For the gambler, the saying is, "I feel, therefore I am". Thus the gambler confirms his existence by arousing feelings within himself. A final piece of evidence for the theory that gambling confirms our existence comes from a race track gambler who was recently interviewed. He said:

"You ask me why I gamble and I tell you, it's the thrill. I know the game is crooked and that I haven't a chance, but when I've put my money on the horse and hear its name on the speaker, my heart stands still, I know I am alive."

How does gambling affirm our worth? Gambling affirms our worth by eliciting positive emotions about ourselves. When we gamble and we win we can feel emotions such as pride, courage, and self-esteem. Doctor Kusyszyn's research has shown that when gamblers are actually engaged in the act of gambling they feel happy, thrilled, excited, powerful, brave, and like a hero. The gamblers also reported feeling full of energy, in control of the situation, and confident of winning. One gambler who had just picked a winner at the race track provides a final piece of evidence for the theory that gambling affirms our worth. This gambler's friends were making fun of him and accused him of picking the winner by luck. The gambler answered, "Luck my ass. Who do you think I am, a nobody?"

Gambling As An Altered State of Consciousness

There is more to the psychology of gambling than the need to confirm the gambler's existence and affirm his worth. The most attractive feature of gambling is its ability to put us into an altered state of consciousness. It is this altered state of consciousness which is the addicting property of gambling. Gambling releases us from the real world. The gambler, very quickly, usually as soon as he begins to contemplate his first wager, transports himself into a play world, a fantasy world in which he stays suspended until he is jarred back into reality by the disappearance of all of his money. While on this mental midway he acts, feels, and thinks with abandon. He suspends himself at a comfortable level of arousal. He is "high" or spaced out. While in this altered state of consciousness he can courageously test his decision-making and predictive powers by trying to guess what to bet on and what bet will win, and in this way he gains a glimpse of his real unconscious self. Gambling allows the gambler to be an actor, not merely an actor, but the hero of his own little drama.

It is the placing of the wager which provides for the placing of the self in the hands of risk and uncertainty. The uncertainty of the game and the risk that is an integral part of it provide for the cognitive-emotional-muscular arousal of the individual. The arousal coupled with the already affirmed belief that the situation is a safe one (because it is only play) free from the possibility of real failures and real punishments from society, leave the gambler in a very comfortable state - in a released or selfless state. This state may be spoken of as a mood state, as a "high", as a"peak"experience as a trance, as a trip, as a spiritual or mystical state, as a religious experience or most commonly as an altered state of consciousness. It is this state that is most addicting for the gambler. This state can be reached in many other ways besides gambling. Any activity that can be labelled play can put you into this state. For example, Dr. Kusysyzn believes that the strongest human motive is to play and not to work. Work came many thousands of years after play in the evolution of man. The natural biological need of humans is to play. Play is an instinct that is always seeking fulfillment and can never be eradicated. Although society frowns on adults playing, adults do in fact play in a number of disguised ways. For example, they play music; they go to see plays; they play cards; they play games; they play sports; they play the stock market. They play around; sometimes they play with themselves; they engage in foreplay, sexplay, and horseplay. They also play the horses, or they may play bingo; pun is a play on words and so on. Why do people play? To reach an altered state of consciousness.

Casino administrators are the best applied psychologists in the world. Every casino operator knows how to put his clients into an altered state of consciousness so that he will lose his money very smoothly, easily, and without any complaints. Gamblers can be helped into an altered state of consciousness by giving them an ego massage (that is by praising them and calling them Mr. or Sir). Gamblers can also be put into an altered state of consciousness with alcohol, with gourmet meals, and with musical or comical entertainment. If you want to gamble professionally you must be aware of the strong attraction to altered states of consciousness. The way to battle getting into this state is to have a game plan and to know what to do ahead of time before you enter the state. The chapter in this book on THE THEORY OF THE PROFESSIONAL GAMBLER is designed to keep the gambler working towards his goal of making money and away from the possibility of flipping into an altered state of consciousness.

Write to Dr. Kusysyzn in the Psychology Department at York University in Toronto, Canada if you are interested in the psychology of gambling and wish to obtain literature on it. Dr. Kusysyzn has a nine hundred item bibliography listing almost every study and book ever performed and written on the psychology of gambling.

18   THE JUNKET

Here I go again! I am about to take off on my thirty-
first junket to Las Vegas. I made one phone call two weeks ago
and I'm on. All I have to do now is show up at the airport on
Wednesday at 10 in the morning. Absolutely everything has been
arranged for me. My plane ticket will be waiting at the airport.
A seat will have been especially reserved on the charter just for
me. My baggage will be automatically tagged and taken care of
by Max the junket runner. A room has already been assigned to me
at the Strand Hotel and Casino in Vegas. I will get a VIP personal
credit card, compliments of the casino, on arrival. This card
will allow me to see any and every show free of charge in the hotel.
The card will also allow me to eat in every cafe and restaurant on
the premises free of charge. It will also pay for any guest I may
wish to entertain, male or female. The card will also permit me to
order anything I may want to be sent up to my room - steaks, liquor,
complete gourmet dinners, etc. Most importantly the card will
allow me to simply sign for $5,000.00 worth of casino chips to
gamble with. That one thin, little, insignificant-looking plastic
card will get me everything I mentioned for free. All I have to do
is sign, and of course, obtain the card in the first place.

You are probably wondering how I rate such a card in the
first place. Maybe you're thinking something like, "If he can get
one maybe I can too." So you want to know how I rate? O.K. Let
me begin at the beginning.

Just six years ago, in 1970, I had never been inside a casino
in my life. I was just a guy practising my profession, which was
teaching psychology at a university, and engaging in what was then
my favourite hobby - betting the harness races. I actually won at
the races with a semi-scientific method which I developed after
watching thousands of races and reading every book published on the
harness races. My success achieved notoriety and a story along
with a photograph of my unshaven face (half a page of it) appeared in

the magazine supplement to the Saturday edition of a large newspaper. The story stated that I was ahead of the game about $3,000 on the year up to that time.

To make a long story short, the newspaper story appeared on Saturday. On Monday morning I found three freshmen parked outside my office door. You will never believe what they wanted. You can probably guess it. Yes, they did. They wanted me to begin offering a course on gambling! They read about my method and success, and wanted to learn how to beat the races themselves. Naturally, I laughed at their idea. Who everheard of a university course on gambling? Nobody. The mere thought of such a thing is preposterous, I thought then. However, by the end of the week the university was flooded with telephone calls from people of all ages who wanted to know whether the professor was offering a course in gambling. The demand was so great that the university's extension department asked me whether I could mount such a course. I said I thought I could but I would need some time to organize the table of contents and plan the lectures. They gave me four weeks. I made the deadline.

The first class had only 15 students. (The second class held eight weeks later had 90! Why? Because I took the first class to the track on a "field trip" and between us we won over $900 in that one night. The story made the papers. Need I say more?) I learned more from the 15 students about gambling than they learned from me. A lot of them were gambling veterans. Several of them had been going to Las Vegas for years and they had all been losing. Others spent five, ten, some more than twenty years at the racetracks. They all wanted me to teach them how to win. Now that was no problem for me as far as the races were concerned. But what did I know about craps or blackjack? Let me tell you all I knew about these games then: I knew that one was dice and the other had to do with cards. That's all! Hard to believe, isn't it? It's true. But luckily I am a fast learner - after all it is my profession - I learned much about craps from Scarne's books and much about blackjack from Thorp's Beat the Dealer. And I taught the students the theory of craps and the theory of blackjack. In the middle of one of my lectures a very

strange thing happened. One of the students, Len, who was about 50,
said out loud that I didn't know what I was talking about. I was
stunned. My face went red. I became speechless. No one had ever
told me, the professor, that I did not know what I was talking about.
Len said, "I bet you've never even been in a casino." I admitted
that I had not. "It's different when you start playing, it's not
like in the book. You can read all the books you want and they won't
help you in a casino unless you know what to do from experience." he
said. I agreed. At this point, Terry, one of the other students
who was about 40, came to my rescue and said that he would take me
on a junket to Las Vegas with him so that I could test my theory of
blackjack. I agreed to go. But I wanted to go as a regular junketeer
- as a player - and not as a guest. Here is how I had to go about
establishing CREDIT to become eligible to go with all expenses paid.
This is where the story of THE JUNKET really begins.

The rule is that you must first be RECOMMENDED by a player who
is already an established junket gambler. Terry was such a person.
He is a salesman who goes down two or three times a year. His credit
is good. This means on the occasions he lost money his cheque was
always good. Terry recommended me to Max who is a travel agent who
travels mainly on junkets. And why not. Max gets $50 per player per
trip. Multiply that by about 100 players and note that he makes two
trips a month. It is a very lucrative business indeed.

I got Max's phone number from Terry, called him and told him
I wanted to go on the next trip. He told me to talk to my bank manager
and to get him to send him a letter stating that I had credit for
$3,000 (the sum if $5,000 now due to inflation and other things like greed
on the part of the casinos). Credit for $3,000 means that should I
lose that much the bank would guarantee that my cheque would be good.
Luckily I had an understanding bank manager and the credit was arranged.
Some bank managers are less hospitable. They actually want you to take
out a loan for the amount of credit you want with the junket people.

The arranging of credit is the most critical part of becoming
a regular on the junket lists. Once you have established credit in
one casino (through your travel agent) then you can establish credit in
almost any other casino in Las Vegas or in the world. All you have to

do is fill out an application card. The new casino will check your
credit with your old casino or with Central Credit (Central Credit
is an agency that has credit information on every person that
ever had credit in any casino in the world. Frightening isn't it?)
When the new casino gets the information it is looking for, which
is simply that every cheque you ever wrote for a casino was a good
one and not of rubber variety, you are automatically granted credit
for the same amount as your original sum. The application card for
credit may be easily obtained at the cashier's cage of the casino or
from the travel agent in your home town who runs junkets to that
particular casino. In fact, you will probably be getting such
applications in the mail right after you get back from your first
junket. You see in Las Vegas news travels fast, Central Credit will
know you were there and they can inform all their clients.

Let me now talk about what is required of you as a player on
a junket. In 1976 you are required to make $25 minimum wagers. That
is, every single bet you make in the casino must be a $25 bet or
larger. (In 1970 the minimum bet was only $5). Secondly, you are
expected to gamble at least several hours a day. Thirdly, they
like you to use all of your credit. That is, they like you to use
your credit, $500 or $1000 at a time, per gambling session and to
keep on drawing such amounts until you have drawn out your whole
amount of $3,000 or $5,000 or whatever your credit line may be.
Please don't misunderstand me. They don't expect you to lose your
entire $3,000. All they want you to do is gamble with it for an
appreciable length of time. They know that you are sure to lose a
large chunk of it if you are like the average junketeer. In fact,
according to their experience with house percentages, you will
probably lose at least twnety percent of the amount. This is known
as 20% of the DROP.

O.K., so now I know what is expected of me. What if I lose
my first $500, get scared, and refuse to lose any more? What if I
stop gambling? What will they do to me? This is a very important
question. Most of the time they will do absolutely nothing to you.
The travel agent will simply put your name down very low on his

priority list so that the next time you call him asking to go on the junket he will simply say that he has no room. If you believe him and decide to wait until the next trip to call him he will tell you the same thing. If you persist and tell him that you really want to get on the junket he may be kind to you and tell you that the casino felt you did not "use your credit enough" last time. And if you give him your word to use all of your credit he will telephone the casino (Long Distance yet!) and inform them of this. They may give you another chance, he says. It's out of his hands. It's up to them, he says. He'll try to convince them that you are a "good" player. He is on your side, etc., etc., etc. The likely outcome of this exchange is that nine times out of ten you will get on the junket. You see, they don't want to lose a customer. After all, on this trip you may get drunk and lose your entire $3,000. This will more than make up for your first fiasco. They make it very easy to lose very much very comfortably. The atmosphere of every casino is purposedly engineered, and I do mean ENGINEERED, to draw your chips from you. The cocktails, the cocktail waitresses, the courteous dealers, the deferring pit bosses, the dim hypnotizing lighting, the easy come-easy go attitude about the chips, the round the clock gambling, the glamour attached to the idea of being a VIP - a big shot who gets everything free and so on.

Many blackjack players will not go on a junket because they say they are under too much pressure to gamble. They do not want to gamble $3,000 or $5,000 worth of chips even if they can afford to. They choose to bide their time and pick their own casinos from among the 35 in Las Vegas. If you cannot stand the pressure of junket gambling I recommend that you also pay your own way and play where you like. I personally do not like to go to certain casinos on a junket because of the pressure. Foreign casinos are the worst for pressure because they make you cash in your chips (if you have any left) after each playing session.

Please don't let me scare you. I am not putting junkets
down. After all, I am about to go on my thirty-first one. Some
people have learned how to survive and even how to profit on a
junket. Others get buried every time they go. These latter souls
are most often craps players. You see, over a four or five day period
of craps shooting, it is simply impossible to come out a winner.
The house percentages in craps will not permit it. There are rare
exceptions. These are as rare as a person surviving a twenty storey
fall. There is only one way to survive on a junket and that is to
learn how to play blackjack. You need not learn how to play professionally. All you need to learn is enough to get the percentages
on your side. Way back in 1970, I taught myself how to play blackjack
well enough to win the first five times I went on junkets. Then
the roof fell in on the sixth trip. Let me tell you about it.

On the sixth trip, they found out I was a COUNTER. After
the sixth trip I never won in that casino again. I was using at
that time a simple point count along with the basic strategy as
described in Thorp's book Beat the Dealer. At first my betting was
in direct proportion to the running count. That is, at a count of
plus one I bet one chip, at plus two, I bet two chips, at plus three
I bet three chips, and so on. After coming home a winner from the
first three trips, I began to bet more boldly. By the sixth trip I
was ranging my bets between a $5 minimum bet and a $150 maximum bet,
betting two hands at $75 a hand. I was doing this in a single deck
game at the Gobi casino. I didn't know the pit bosses don't like
a player to range his bets in this way. I didn't know you weren't
supposed to win on a junket. I thought all they wanted from a junket
player was action. I gave them plenty of action. I would play at
least 10 hours every single day.

After the first few trips to the Gobi, I weeded out the
tough dealers from the easy dealers. I did not believe at that time
there was cheating in Las Vegas. Even though I did read about the
cheating in Thorp's book, I thought that they only cheated people who
bet a lot of money or who were a big threat to them. I never thought

they would cheat me. At any rate, after discovering who the tough
and the easy dealers were, I stayed away from the tough dealers and
only played against the easy dealers. Looking back on it, this was
probably why I was so successful in winning. There were two dealers
that were exceptionally good to play against in the Gobi, Ron and
Mike. Ron still deals in the Gobi today, but Mike is now a pit boss
at the Stilton. I was playing against Mike when I was betting my
$5 to $150 that I was talking about above. One of the pit bosses
rushed over and told Mike to shuffle up. This was when I had two
$75 bets out. Mike shuffled up and I started with my $5 bet again
off the top of the new deck. I kept on playing and the count became
positive, so I put $150 out there again. By this time, the pit boss
walked over to the head pit boss that was standing by the desk in
the centre of the pit and started talking about me. I knew they were
talking about me because they were both looking at me and the big
pit boss got red in the face and began to shake. I didn't pay too
much attention to it, I just kept on playing and winning. The next
thing I saw was the head pit boss coming over to my table with the
manager of the casino. The manager was a very nice gentlemen with
a dark blue suit and wavy grey hair. I knew him because he had made
several show reservations in other casinos on previous trips. As
he came over to the table I said "Hi, how are you?" He said, "Hello",
that's all, but he was very pleasant and he just stayed for a minute
and looked and then walked away with the head pit boss. I thought
nothing of it at the time. I had won enough that day so I didn't
play anymore and the next morning was the final morning of the junket.
I was up money so I usually make it a rule not to play on the final
morning. This is because I am usually quite tired from the four days
of playing. However, this time I thought I would just take out
$200 and play long enough to win $125 because I wanted to buy a radio
for my car. However, my favorite dealers Mike and Ron didn't start
work until 12 noon, therefore, I had to play against other dealers.
I tried three different dealers and couldn't win against any of them.
I lost almost my entire $200. The last dealer I was playing against
was R.B. These were the initials on his tie. I remembered that he was
one of the tougher dealers. As he began to take my money he told
me to take it easy, that I had won enough this trip. I didn't realize
how good his advice was and that he was actually trying to help me.

Because, you see, I had been pointed out to him and to the other dealers as a counter. And the dealers were instructed not to let me win anymore. As I said before, I have never won in this casino since that time. I rarely play there now. I go in about once a year but I am recognized within the first few minutes that I sit down.

What can you learn from my junket story? The moral is not to give yourself away as a winning player. Junkets are fine to go on if you know how to handle yourself. The advice given in the rest of this book should be sufficient to teach you how to gamble successfully while on a junket and get all your expenses paid for while walking away with the casino's money.

19   BLACKJACK BITS

The purpose of this chapter is to compile bits of information
which did not appear in the text of the book. These are extra
pieces of information that the player should find helpful in improving
his knowledge of the game. They were not put into the body of the
book either because they didn't quite fit in any particular chapter
or because I simply forgot them at that time. The separate pieces
of information can easily be identified by their sub-headings. The
information is in no particular order.

The burn card and the bottom card

The player can gain an extra advantage if he can get a glimpse
of the burn card and/or the bottom card. The burn card is the card
which the dealer burns. By burning is meant putting the card out of
play. The burn card is always the card on the top of the deck after
the deck has been shuffled and cut. After the deck has been shuffled
by the dealer and cut by one of the players, the dealer takes the top
card and places it on the bottom of the deck face up to cover up the
bottom card. This is what he does with the burn card when he is
dealing a one or a two deck game out of the hand. When the game is
a shoe game the dealer takes the top card and simply places it in the
discard rack. It is almost impossible to get a glimpse of the burn
card in a shoe game because the dealer simply takes the card out of
the shoe and slides it face down on top of the table over the discard
rack. However, in a one or two deck game dealt out of the hand, the
player can get a look at the burn card and also at the card on the
bottom of the deck if he sits in a seat which is at the proper angle
to the dealer. The best seat is either the second seat at the table
or the second last seat at the table. In general, I recommend sitting
in the second last seat for other reasons described in the book.
Therefore, this is where you should sit for this purpose also. When

sitting in the second last seat you are viewing the deck at an
approximately 45 degree angle. This is the optimum angle in order
to get a glimpse of the burn card or the bottom card when the dealer
is in the process of burning the burn card. It is rare that you are
able to see both the burn card and the bottom card from one seat at
the table. You usually see either the burn card or the bottom card
depending on which side of the table you are sitting on and also
depending on whether the dealer is left-handed or right-handed. The
advantage of seeing either one of the two cards comes from the fact
that you have seen an extra card or two and have counted it as either
a plus or a minus (or sometimes as a zero) value. Should one of
these two cards turn out to be a plus card, then you automatically have
the advantage and can place a large wager right at the top of a one
deck game. Should it be a negative value card, then you can place
your minimum wager.

Cutting the deck

There are certain ways to cut the deck which can add to your
advantage. These ways can be taken advantage of most when you are
playing alone against the dealer. For example, if you are sitting
in the second last seat trying to see the dealer's burn card or bottom
card and you find that you can't see them because he has turned
slightly in order to face you (most dealers do turn their bodies in
order to face the only player at their table because this makes it
easier for them to deal, otherwise they would be dealing sideways),
you can get the dealer to twist his body around to a more favourable
angle for you to be able to see either the burn card or the bottom
card by the way you cut the deck. Here is how to do it. When he gives
you the deck to cut, then just take half of it, but don't put the half
you picked up right beside the other half that is lying on the table.
Put it about a foot away from the other half of the deck. This move
forces the dealer to move his arms and most of the time also twist his
body in order to pick up the other half of the deck. Consequently, when
he puts the two halves together, he is not quite in the same position as
he was before. That is, with your cut you have changed the angle at

which he is holding the deck in relation to your visual perspective.
You have to experiment on exactly which side to place your half of
the deck after you have cut it with different dealers, in order to
get them to move around.

Another very important move in cutting the deck has to do with
cutting the deck so that it automatically becomes advantageous to you.
In order to get the deck to be advantageous to you, the thing to do
is to cut the deck where it resists cutting. Do not cut the deck where
it wants to be cut. You will find in most decks that there are certain
places in the deck where it is easy to cut the deck. In these places
one of the cards is bent and therefore creates a larger space between
it and the adjoing cards than would normally be the case. The bent
cards are usually ten-value cards or aces. Why? Because these are
the cards that are bent when they are the dealer's up cards. He bends
these cards of course, in order to have a look at his bottom card to see
whether he has a blackjack. These gaps in the deck caused by ten value
cards and aces are quite prominent if the deck is not a new deck.
If you are not aware of this cutting move which I am describing you would
probably cut where the deck is easiest to cut and therefore put a ten
or an ace on the bottom of the deck! This of course would put that good
card out of play. That is, if you should see this card your count would
now be minus one which is not favourable to you. Conversely, if you
cut the deck where it resists cutting you will probably cut a small
card to the bottom of the deck. And, as you know, a small card is an
advantageous card for you to have out of play.

There is also an advantage which can be gained by cutting in a
shoe game. The cut to be described is used in conjunction with the
final card count at the shuffle point. That is, if you are keeping a
running count of all the cards in the shoe from the time the dealer begins
dealing to the time he hits the plastic marker card you will wind up with
a plus count about 50% of the time. What this means is that the cards
which are left in the shoe (this means approximately 50 cards) are
advantageous to you because the plus count that you ended up with means
that there are more ten-value cards in those cards which were left in
the shoe and not dealt. Keep your eye on these remaining undealt cards.
Follow that clump of cards through the dealer's entire shuffle. You

will see that that clump of cards will be shuffled into half of the
remaining cards. The dealers in the state of Nevada are all taught
to deal the shoe in one specific way. They do not shuffle the shoe
as thoroughly as it could be shuffled. Therefore, the undealt clump
is only shuffled into half of the cards that were dealt out. What
this means is that the positive count which you originally ended up
with stays in half of the shoe. Therefore, the thing to do is to
divide the count you were left with by two in order to get a more
accurate picture of the count in that particular half of the shoe.
All this is done while the dealer is shuffling all of the cards. Now
the cutting part comes in. The dealer puts all the cards together
and he gives you the plastic marker to cut with. The thing to do is
to cut the cards anywhere you like but make sure you know where the
plus count cards are. The ideal way to cut is to cut the cards in
such a way as to bring the positive part of the decks to the front so
that when the dealer begins dealing the count is plus right at the top
of the deck. The thing to do here of course is to make large wagers
right off the top of the deck. Then after several hands have been
played you have to watch how many cards have been dealt out to know
how to adjust your count in order to take into account the fact that
a lot of ten-value cards have already been dealt out. The procedure
just described is an advanced procedure in blackjack play. It takes
some practice in order to perfect. My description of it is more
complicated than the procedure actually is.

Mixing your chips

One way to camouflage the amount of money you are betting is
to mix your chips. By mixing your chips I mean putting chips of
different denominations all into one betting pile. The best way to
do this is to have a pile of chips with at least five chips in it.
When you are betting a small amount you'd have four of the five chips
being   dollar chips and the remaining one could be a five dollar chip
for a total of $9. When you are making a large bet you could still
only have five chips up there but three of the five could be five
dollar chips and the other two one dollar chips for a total of $17.
If a pit boss is watching from a distance it will be harder than usual

for him to tell that you have raised your bet because your pile is
not any higher than it usually is. The only problem with this camouflage technique is that some dealers don't like it when you mix chips
because it means more work for them sorting out the chips when they
have to pay you. You can very easily smooth this problem over by
tipping the dealer.

The team approach to the shoe game

Over the years a number of teams have won substantial amounts
of money playing against the shoe. There are several advantages of
the team approach. Here is how to use the approach. Two or more
people walk into the same casino from different entrances and sit down
at different tables and begin playing. Each person continues to play
until one of two things happen.   If the count turns negative, the
person quits, gets up and starts walking around the table watching
his team members. If the count turns positive the person at that high
positive table signals his other team members. The other team members
come to his   table and start making large wagers taking advantage
of the large positive count. That is essentially the team approach.
The purpose of it is not to waste time playing when the count is
negative.   A second advantage of this approach is that a smaller overall
bankroll is required when different members are playing at high
positive counts at different tables. This second advantage applies
more to a large team.

Disguises

Should you be barred from a casino, don't worry about it, there
are ways to get back and play in that casino again. Here are some
of them. First of all, a player is rarely barred from all three shifts
in that casino. Usually he is barred by one shift boss from playing
on that particular shift. Thus he can go into the casino on the other
two shifts and not be bothered, unless of course one of the pit bosses
happens to be working on the two different shifts and spots him.
Another way to get around the idea of being barred is to first of all
stay away from that particular casino for at least six months and
then secondly, when you come back, come back disguised. The best kind

of a disguise involves a total transformation. By total transformation I mean changing the length of your hair, changing the colour
of your hair, changing the style of your clothing, changing the tone
of your voice, or talking a lot the second time back if you were
quiet the first time or vice-versa. The total transformation also
involves betting different colored chips and sitting in a different
seat at the table.

Talk to the pit boss before playing

Dealers are usually afraid of or respectful of the floor men
or the pit bosses they work with. Dealers must respect these people
even though they may not like them because they could lose their
jobs if the bosses don't like the way they deal. Because of this
interpersonal situation, some of the professional blackjack players
get to know the pit bosses and are sure to speak to them when they
come into the casino before they sit down to play. If you should do
this the dealerswill see you talking to the pit bosses and they will
think twice about cheating you or shuffling up on you. I have done
this in several casinos and it worked for me almost every single time.

The advantages of being female

Mr. Lawrence Revere, author of Playing Blackjack as a Business
states in his book that a woman who learns how to play winning blackjack can win a million dollars by virtue of being a female. I have
found this statement to be true in Las Vegas. In general, Las Vegas
casino administrators do not respect women as gamblers. They do not
feel that a woman has the mentality or the inclination to be a professional blackjack player. If you are a woman and like to play blackjack
you have a very, very profitable future ahead of you. I know some
men players who disguise themselves as women to take advantage of this
situation.

Gambling is good for you

In the chapter on the PSYCHOLOGY OF GAMBLING I forgot to mention
that for most people gambling is a natural and a healthy activity. My
students and I did a race track study in which we found that the average
person spends 22 hours per week gambling, playing the horses. This
seems like a lot of time to spend at a race track. And one would think

that people who spend this much time at a race track are probably
sick, compulsive gamblers. We found the opposite to be true. We
found that these people were psychologically more healthy than people
who do not gamble. They were found to have happier family lives,
they were also found to be less hostile and to be less anxious and
neurotic than the comparison group of people. Therefore, gambling is
healthy for people who already gamble. I am not suggesting that if
you do not gamble that you begin gambling in order to get healthy.
What I am saying is that people who gamble have been found to be at
least as healthy if not more healthy psychologically than people who
do not gamble. Therefore, if you like to gamble don't be ashamed of
it, continue to gamble as long as gambling continues to add pleasure
and excitement to your life. However, do not go to extremes and become
an excessive gambler. If you begin to gamble excessively, you will
find you are enjoying it less and your friends and relatives will be
enjoying you less as well. Any activity engaged in to excess is
psychologically harmful.

Play alone

Many people who come to Las Vegas come with a friend. This
is fine. Then they walk around together and play together at the same
table. This is not fine and should be avoided. You should never mix
socializing with gambling. I have found over and over again that a
friend playing at my table influences my game. He either asks for help
or wants to quit before I do, or wants to stay and play longer than I do
etc, etc. Play alone. Rudyard Kipling said, "He travels the fastest
who travels alone". Take his word for it.

Adopt a spy mentality

One method that some players use successfully can be compared
to playing the role of a spy. What is a spy like? A spy is unobtrusive.
He doesn't bother anybody. He is quiet, and polite. He looks like the
natives, he dresses like the natives, and he talks like the natives.
He never stands out. He pretends to have the same values as the natives.
He likes money and he likes women. He follows at least one sport and
he's up on politics. The spy is also extremely well-trained for his job.

However, he is trained so well that the training never shows. He looks casual but his brain is functioning at a very rapid rate. He is aware of everything that is going on around him at all times. He uses his training, his experience, and his determination to get the job done. And the job is to win a lot of money in the casino without anyone knowing how much was taken out.

Your bet range

Some players have asked me, "What is more important - the playing strategy or money management?" That is, is it more important to play accurately or to bet accurately? The answer is that betting is much more important than how you play. The greater the range of your bets the more money you will win per hour. If you can camouflage your bets so that you can range one to eight or higher you will win at a very quick rate no matter what playing strategy you use. Therefore the bet range is very important for winning money quickly. Even if you play only basic strategy and even if you play incorrect basic strategy you can still win money by ranging your bets from at least one to eight. Of course, the more accurate and the more powerful your playing strategy the better it is. However, any inaccuracies or lack of power in the playing strategy can easily be compensated for by increasing the range of your bets. This is a very fortunate circumstance because it is much easier to bet than it is to learn how to play correctly.

Hide your winnings

If you are skilful with your hands it is a good idea to hide as many chips as you can from your winnings. There are a number of ways to go about doing this. One thing you can do is to get the smaller denominations changed into larger chips so that it will look to the pit boss as though you've got fewer chips in front of you. You can even hide some of the larger chips such as the $25 dollar chips with smaller chips such as $5 and $1 chips. Another thing to do is to simply pick up several large denomination chips and slip them into your shirt pocket when the pit boss isn't looking. One technique that I have found to be successful when I am on a junket and required to draw $500 worth of chips at a time is switch tables and as I am walking from one table to the next with several hundred dollars worth of chips in my hands I just put a few in my sports jacket pocket. It's very difficult for the pit boss or the dealer to notice what you are doing when you are walking or hopping from table to table.

Decks with a border

You have probably noticed that very few casinos in Nevada use bridge decks in their blackjack games. A bridge deck is a deck that has a border around it. It is quite easy to see someone cheating when they are using a deck with a border around it. It is particularly easy to spot the dealing of seconds with a border deck. This is because you can see that the top card isn't moving by virtue of the fact that it does have a border around it and when the second card comes out the difference between the border and the rest of the card contrasted with the top card becomes very apparent. The cards that are used in the blackjack games in Las Vegas do not have a border around them, with the exception of one or two casinos. With no borders it is very difficult to tell whether you are getting the top card dealt to you or some other card. Since dealing seconds is the most common way of cheating you may be interested in learning more about this practice. If you are consult the books on my recommended list authored by Livingston, Roberts, and Noir. The books by those authors have photographs of dealers peeking and dealing seconds.

Playing two or more hands

Many players ask me, "Should I play two hands"? It depends. In general, you are better off to play only one hand. When you play two hands the best time to do it would be when you have the advantage, naturally. In this way you could bet twice as much money and then win of course at twice the rate. However, you can also bet twice as much money on one hand. So why play two hands? Some players believe that playing two hands offers them more protection against losing because usually one hand cancels out the other hand. According to Professor Epstein this is only true about 25% of the time. That is, if you are going to

lose you'll lose both hands 75 % of the time and if you are going to
win you're going to win both hands 75% of the time. However, the
real disadvantage of playing two or more hands is that you are using
up the deck unnecessarily. Why use up a good positive deck by playing
extra hands when you can bet more money on one hand and in this way
get more good, positive hands out of the deck. I do not recommend that
you play two hands against a single or double deck game. You can play
two hands in a four deck game if you are ranging your bets from one to
sixteen or one to twenty-four or even one to thirty-two. By playing
more hands it is easier to camouflage your range.

In the four deck game there is also another completely different
situation in which more than one hand is recommended. This is near
the beginning of the game when you are encountering a negative count.
You can get rid of the negative count faster by playing   two, three,
four, five, six, or seven handsusing an absolute minimum on each hand.
That is, if you want to get rid of the negative count fast, simply play
more hands to get a lot of cards out of that shoe fast. I only recommend this practice when you can do it using one dollar chips. If you
are a player who ranges his bets from $2 to $32 or from $1 to $32, as
some players do, then you could try this practice. If you are a primarily
$5 a chip bettor then you would have to be ranging your bets at least
$5 to $80 if you are going to use this practice of betting $5 on several
hands in order to get rid of the negative count. If your range is smaller
it would not be worth your while in the long run to waste your money in
this way. You would be losing, of course, more times than winning, on
a negative count.

Pick your dealer carefully

If you were to ask me what the most important single element was
in winning at blackjack I would have to say that it is your choice of
the dealer. You must learn how to choose an honest dealer. If you can
not identify honest dealers you will never win any appreciable money in
blackjack. The second most important thing to winning at blackjack is
the bet range, which was discussed above.

Control over emotions

Many players lose because they become emotionally involved in the game. When they are losing they become emotionally aroused and start steaming. They begin to chase their losses. There is a trick which you can learn which will help you control yourself. It has simply to do with paying attention to your emotions. As soon as you feel yourself getting emotionally aroused, stop and allow the emotional arousal to act as a signal for you to quit. This will take you several playing sessions to master. However, once mastered, it will save you hundreds and thousands of dollars in your lifetime.

Casinos with favourable rules

The two most common favourable rules for the player are Surrender and Doubling After Splitting. At the writing of this book, the following Las Vegas casinos allow you to surrender: Caesar's Palace, Dunes, Riviera, Thunderbird, El Cortez, Landmark and the Las Vegas Club. Also at this writing the following casinos allow you to double your bet after pair splitting: Caesar's Palace, Four Queens , Hacienda, El Cortez, Frontier, MGM Grand, Paradise. See Table DK-RS on the next page for more information.

Get change immediately for tipping

It is an excellent practice to, as soon as you sit down at the table, and while you are buying your chips, take one of your chips and get it changed into smaller chips. The dealer will automatically know that the reason you asked for the change was because you plan to make some bets for him during the game. He will automatically know that you are going to look after him. If he is a cheating dealer he is less likely to cheat you when you do this.

The blackjack dealer

One way to spot a cheating dealer is by watching to see if he deals himself a blackjack after he shuffles. Many more Strip dealers will be found to deal themselves a blackjack right off the top than Downtown dealers. If you find that a dealer deals himself a blackjack as soon as you sit down to play against him, I recommend that you get up again.

TABLE DK-RS: DECK AND RULES VARIATIONS IN LAS VEGAS AS OF SEPTEMBER 1976

DECKS	Number of Tables Dealing-Number of Decks Shown			Total Number of Tables	Double After Split (X = Yes)	Surrender (X = Yes)	Resplit Aces (X = Yes)	
	1	2	4					
Aladdin		21	19	40				2 Deck Down: 4 Deck Up
Caesar's Palace	2		29	31	X	X		1 Deck Down: 4 Deck Up
Castaways	9			9				All Face Down
Circus Circus	44			44				All Single Deck: Face Down
Desert Inn			16	16			X	All Face Up
Dunes	16		11	27		X		1 Deck Down: 4 Deck Up
El Cortez	13	8	1	22	X	X	X	4 Deck Up: Rest Down
Flamingo	9	9		18				All Face Down
Fremont	2	6	31	39				All Face Down
4 Queens	12	24		36	X		X	All Face Down
Frontier			20	20	X			All Face Up
Golden Gate	15	1		16				All Face Down
Golden Nugget		22	11	33				All Face Down
Hacienda	11	11	11	33	X			All Face Down
Hilton	30			30				All Face Down
Holiday Inn			30	30				All Face Down
Horseshoe	23		1	24			X	1 Deck Face Down: 4 Deck Up
Jackpot	4		4	8				1 Deck Face Down: 4 Deck Up
Landmark	11		7	18	X			All Face Down
Marina	10		20	30				All Face Down
MGM Grand			61	61	X			All Face Down
Mint	5	15	17	37				All Face Down
Paradise	8			8	X			All Face Down
Riviera		31		31		X		All Face Down
Royal Inn	11			11				All Face Down
Royal L.V.	3	3	1	7				4 Deck Face Up: Rest Down
Sahara	20		4	24				All Face Down
Sands			22	22				All Face Down
Silver Slipper	2	11		13				All Face Down
Stardust	4	4	39	47				1 Deck Face Down: 2 & 4 Decks Face Up
T-Bird		11	4	15		X		All Face Down
Tropicana			20	20				All Face Down
Union Plaza		17	12	29				All Face Down

How much should I bet for the dealer?

The recommendations for betting the dealer are as follows. If you are betting five dollar chips then make only one dollar bets for the dealer. If you are only winning a little bit, just make one or two one dollar bets for him. However, if you are winning a lot you can make four, five, six or seven one dollar bets for him. If you are playing with $25 chips, then you should use $5 chips to bet for the dealer. With one hundred dollar chips it is customary to use $25 chips to bet for the dealer.

The CUT-OFF dealer

Do not play against the dealer that cuts off more than half the deck or the shoe. You either will have no mathematical advantage or such a small advantage that it won't be worth your while.

Quitting for the day

Should you lose against three dealers in one day all in a row, quit either for the day or for a few hours. It is difficult to stay emotionally calm when one is losing against dealer, after dealer, after dealer. The best practice is to simply quit for the day.

Never quit when you are winning. Stay and bet more and more money when you are winning. Go against all of your rules when you are winning. Keep playing while you are winning under any or all unfavourable conditions. Only stop playing when you begin to lose.

Don't turn your head

Don't turn your head while you are playing. This may sound like a trivial piece of advice. However, what if somebody walks up and bumps into you while they are sitting down? Ninety-nine out of a hundred players will turn their head to see who the person is. You should train yourself not to turn around. You should train yourself never to allow your eyes to stray from the deck.

The face-up game

In most European casinos and in the casinos in the Islands they deal the cards face-up. Several casinos in Las Vegas also deal the

cards face-up. It is much easier to keep track of cards when they
deal face-up. I recommend that you always play in a face-up game
whenever you can find one. This kind of a game is also faster than
the face-down game. However, if you follow my instructions on how
to slow down the dealer, you will never have to worry about being
rushed. The face-up game allows you to play very accurately because
you can see all of the players' cards all of the time.

Going to the washroom

If you are playing in a shoe game and you have to go to the
washroom wait until the count is negative before going. Why leave
when the count is positive? I make it a practice to visit the washroom very often when I play in a casino which has shoes. As soon
as the count gets up to minus four or five or higher I just leave and
stay in the washroom as long as I think is necessary for the dealer
to reach the end of the deck. I time my return so that I come back
when he is shuffling the cards.

Keeping separate track of aces

Once you have begun to win money in a casino you are ready to
improve your game by adding certain refinements. One very important
refinement is keeping separate track of aces. If you are playing in
a one or two deck game you can simply use the chips in front of you
to count how many aces have been dealt out of the deck. The general
rule is that for every extra ace that is left in the deck, you can add
a count of plus one to the running count for betting purposes. Conversely, for every extra ace that is out of the deck, you can add a
count of minus one to your running count for betting purposes. For
example, say you have just sat down at a single deck game and have
played one hand and no aces came out. Let us further say that the count
after you have played your hand and the dealer has played his hand, is
zero. Under ordinary circumstances this would be an even game, you
would have no advantage. However, because no aces came out of the deck,
you do in fact have an advantage now. Because there is an extra ace
in there or at least a part of an extra ace if less than a quarter of
the deck has been dealt out. Therefore, you can make a larger bet.

When there is a shortage of aces in the deck, it is a good idea to double down less often with an eight, nine, or a ten. The reason for this is obvious, you are less likely to get an ace on your double down.

The trailer

On one of my trips to Las Vegas I brought a friend who had never been there before. My friend Bob was very curious to learn about the game so he would follow me from casino to casino. He would trail along behind me and usually come into the casino a minute or so after I did. He would find the table at which I was playing and would watch me play from a distance. After I quit playing and left the table he would hang around and try to listen to what the dealer and pit boss were saying. In the Three Kings casino Bob saw the pit boss walk over to the dealer right after I had finished playing and ask him the following: "Did you know that you were dealing to a professional blackjack player?" "He's been in here before, but we don't know what his name is". In the Edsel casino, Bob overheard the pit boss saying, after I had left the table, "How was he?" The dealer answered, "Pretty tough". "How much did he walk away with?" "He took away three greens". Then the pit boss said, "He thinks we don't know who he is. He thinks that he can fool us by wearing the hat." (I used to wear golf caps of various colors to try to disguise my appearance). The pit boss ended up by saying, "We know who he is". If you want to know what the pit boss is saying about you perhaps you can try using a"trailer".

Fear of getting barred

When I first learned how to play winning blackjack I was very much afraid of getting detected as a winning player and getting barred. Every time I sat down at the table I became anxious. Since then I have had many players admit that they felt the same way. Do not be afraid of getting barred. They will only bar you if they cannot cheat you. If you have been losing lately you have no fear whatsoever of getting barred. However, if you are a good enough player to avoid being cheated, and have been winning then you may begin to worry about getting barred.

Tough-looking dealers

You will find a lot of ugly, tough-looking dealers in Las Vegas. I have found that tough looking dealers are more difficult to win money against than good-looking dealers. A lot of the tough-looking dealers look like the bad guys you see in the movies. They look ugly and brutal. I am sure that they repel a lot of players. Why don't the casinos hire only good-looking male and female dealers? I would think it would be much better for their business. The answer is that these tough-looking dealers and other not so tough-looking dealers are probably mobbed-up. The former manager of the Par-O-Dice casino told me in the spring of 1976 that his most difficult problem was trying to get the mobbed-up dealers out of his casino. He said that they were very difficult to get rid of.

Blackjack games in Canada

You can play blackjack games legally in Canada in the province of Alberta. Every year during the month of July there are two hundred blackjack tables open at the Calgary stampede in Calgary, Alberta. The stampede takes place during the first two weeks of July. In the second two weeks of July there are two hundred blackjack tables open at the Edmonton Exhibition. All the games are played using either Las Vegas or Reno rules. The minimum bet is $2 and the maximum bet is only $50. All the games are dealt out of a shoe and are four-deck games. Some dealers deal all the cards out except for about 26 cards. People from the state of Nevada are there to supervise the games but the dealers are local students. The tables are usually crowded.

One good sign of a cheating dealer

Many dealers use the same technique to cheat players when they are dealing a one or two deck game. The method involves winning a player's big wagers when he doubles down. I have found myself losing a lot of large double-down bets when the count is a high plus count by being dealt a small card on my hand of nine, ten, or eleven. It is highly improbable that a person will get a little card on a high plus count. Yet, the cheating dealers find a small card somewhere in the deck to give you when you have a large bet that you doubled down. At the same time they also find one or more small cards for themselves in order to make their hand instead of busting. This second move is also highly improbable on a high plus count. This move is very often used by the dealer when he has a four, five, or six up. Watch for it.

The author's position on dealer cheating

Some casinos are infested with cheaters. Other casinos are relatively free of the lice. Some dealers cheat for the mob, some dealers cheat for the casino, and some dealers cheat for themselves. The final effect of the cheating is the same on the player - his money is stolen. The only way I know to avoid getting cheated is to follow the advice given in this book and to join the International Blackjack Club which publishes up-to-date reports on playing conditions in casinos throughout the world.

The cheating can be eliminated

Professor Edward Thorp suggested a number of excellent ways by which cheating could be eliminated, 15 years ago. His suggestions fell on deaf ears. Cheating could be almost completely eliminated by not allowing the dealer to take a hole card until the players are finished playing and also by dealing only out of the shoe. Most foreign casinos play blackjack in this way. Why hasn't this procedure been adopted in the state of Nevada? Because, if it was the people controlling the operation of blackjack games could not steal money from the absentee casino owners. Even Howard Hughes was robbed. When will the owners wake up to what is going on? Or are they part of the skimming operation?

Memory aids

Some players have trouble memorizing the basic strategy. If you are such a player why not make up a little card half the size of a cigarette package with the basic strategy chart on it and glue it to a cigarette package. Even if you are a non-smoker you can still leave the package on the table in front of you. Some players have charts engraved on cigarette lighters. Dr. Koko Ita lists twenty-one methods of keeping the count in his book. See Recommended Books.

"Heat"

      Heat refers to the pressure put on a winning player by the
pit bosses. Heat can be very uncomfortable for the player. I
received much heat in 1975 while winning in the Silver Pebble. The
Silver Pebble is a casino in Downtown Las Vegas where they are not
used to $25 chip bettors. I was betting $25 chips and was ahead over
$400 when the pit bosses started to buzz around my table. Finally,
they surrounded the table. Two of them stood on each side of the
dealer and two more of them stood behind me, one on either side. This
is called heat. It is a way for the pit bosses to pressure the player
into quitting. If this should happen to you, my advice is to keep
on playing as long as you are winning, in spite of the pressure.

"Help"

      Help refers to the dealer helping the player win by signal-
ing him what his down card is. If you should want to find a dealer
that will "help" you, you must get to know someone in the Las Vegas
underground. There are agents which line up players with dealers.
These agents usually charge 30% of the player's winnings. The 30%
is split between the dealer and the agent, and sometimes also with
the pit boss. I met a high stakes gambler in Las Vegas two years
ago who told me how he got lined up with an agent, who in turn lined
him up with a helping dealer in Lake Tahoe. The dealer was a female.
She and the player worked out a set of signals so that he would know
what the exact identity of each card that she had underneath whenever she had a ten or ace up. The player told me that he played
against the dealer for over three hours and that her signals did in
fact identify every down card correctly to him. He lost $12,000 in
the three hours. Who said there was honor among thieves?

Gambling Conference

The Third Annual Conference on Gambling will be held at
Caesar's Palace December 19-21, 1976. I highly recommend the Conference to anyone interested in the latest computer discoveries
in blackjack. In previous conferences papers were presented (and
distributed free to the audience) by experts such as Professors Thorp,
Griffin, Schneider and Heath. Papers on other gambling subjects
are also presented. There are papers on poker, football, baseball,
the psychology of gambling, the economics of gambling, horseracing,
etc. The Conference is open to the general public. The public is
also invited to submit papers for presentation. For information
write to: Dr. Bill Eadington, Department of Economics, University
of Nevada at Reno, Reno, Nevada 89057.

All the papers that were presented at the First Annual
Conference on Gambling have just been published in book form by
the Charles Thomas Publishing Company. The title of the book is
Gambling and Society. It has 466 pages. It is a beautiful hardcover
volume embossed in gold. It is a collector's item.

20   PERCENTAGE TABLE

The Percentage Table presents the effects of various rules on the player's advantage. The variations assume you are playing basic strategy. Using basic strategy in a single deck game with Las Vegas Strip rules (no doubling after pair splitting; no surrender) your advantage is exactly 0.00 (an even game).

The right hand side of the table contains the advantages gained when using the HI-OPT or HI-OPT II strategies (described in the Appendix) in a single deck game with a 1 to 4 bet range when the dealer deals out 3/4 of the deck.

(A much more detailed account of blackjack percentages will be found in Braun on Blackjack, a book by Julian Braun of IBM, the recognized world authority in computer blackjack. Mr. Braun's book will be available in April of 1977 from International Gaming Incorporated).

Rules Variations	With Basic Strategy	With HI-OPT Strategies
Drawing any number of cards to split aces	+0.14	
Doubling allowed on any 3 cards	+0.19	
Doubling allowed on any number of cards	+0.20	
Surrender	+0.05	+0.25
Doubling allowed after splitting	+0.10	+0.25
Insurance	N/A	+0.20
Flat betting	+0.00	HI-OPT +0.80
Flat betting	+0.00	HI-OPT II +0.95
No resplitting of pairs	-0.05	
No soft doubling	-0.14	
No doubling on 9	-0.14	
No doubling on 10	-0.56	
Four or more decks	-0.54	
Two decks	-0.38	
Dealer hits soft 17	-0.20	
No hole card	-0.13	
Dealer wins ties	-9.00	
Dealer cheats	up to -100.00	up to -100.00

21   RECOMMENDED BOOKS AND PUBLICATIONS

    The following pages contain 16 recommended books and
5 recommended publications. These books and publications will
increase the blackjack player's performance and will also add to
his enjoyment of the game. The outstanding topics covered in each
book will now be briefly pointed out.

    Archer's book is a good, elementary all-round book for the
beginning blackjack player. It is a good first book to begin with
if you know nothing about the game.

    Braun's book is a classic. The blackjack community has
long awaited the publication of this book. Julian Braun is recognized as the world authority on computer blackjack. In this book
he explains in great detail the statistical, mathematical and
probabalistic aspects of blackjack. A wealth of information is
provided for anyone interested in how various blackjack strategies
are derived.

    Collver's book is a very brief but informative paperback.
Collver describes various casinos in the State of Nevada and the
playing conditions there.

    Epstein's book is a book for the mathematically inclined
reader. The book contains much data on the probability of different
gambling games. A very detailed account of the basic strategy and
how it was derived is provided.

    Friedman's book is a very colorful little paperback which
very clearly describes all casino games. This book is very explicit
in how cards are dealt and how payoffs are made by the dealers. This
book is being used by many dealers who are learning how to deal, both
blackjack and craps.

    Fraikin's book is autobiographical. He describes how he was
harassed in Las Vegas because he was winning at the game.

    Ita's book is an informative paperback. It contains complete
instructions on how to win at twenty-one and provides twenty-one
different methods that one can use as aids to counting cards.

    Livingston's book details with the help of photographs the
various methods which are used for cheating at cards.

Noir's book is a serious book on the game of blackjack. It provides a winning strategy and also gives the hourly rate of profit with different methods of play. It contains many illustrations and colored photographs.

The book by Reid and Demarais is a best-seller which gives inside information on the involvement of organized crime in casino gambling.

Revere's book is a very comprehensive volume containing many charts, several winning playing strategies, and various tables indicating the probabilities of winning and losing different kinds of hands. Most of the charts are in color and are easy to learn.

Roberts' book contains a lot of practical information advising the player how to conduct himself in a Las Vegas casino. It also contains a winning strategy.

The book titled Winning At Casino Gaming is an excellent all-round book for casino games. It has a unique chapter in the application of ESP to gambling games. Also it contains,in the Appendix, the latest mathematical developments in computer blackjack.

Edward Thorp's book, Beat the Dealer, is the classic best-seller on the game of blackjack. The original 1962 volume has the important formula to calculate the probability of the gambler's ruin. The revised 1966 volume contains most of the original information plus some new information. This is a very inexpensive paperback. Both volumes have two excellent chapters on cheating on the part of the casino and on casino countermeasures. Both volumes present a no-holds barred, courageous account of blackjack gambling.

Dr. Wilson's book is an excellent book on all casino games. It is especially good for blackjack. It contains a winning strategy and goes into the mathematics of the game in a simple, easy to understand way.

RECOMMENDED BOOKS

Archer, J. The Archer method of winning at 21. Chicago: Henry Regnery Company, 1973.

Braun, J. Braun on blackjack. Toronto: International Gaming Inc. 1977. Address: 25 Johnson Ave., Thornhill, Ontario, Canada L3T 2N8. (Not available until April, 1977).

Collver, D.I. Scientific blackjack and complete casino guide. New York, Arco, 1966, 1971.

Epstein, R.A. The theory of gambling and statistical logic. New York. Academic Press, 1967.

Fraikin, G. L. Inside Nevada gambling. New York: Exposition Press, 1965.

Friedman, B. Casino games. New York: Golden Press, 1973.

Ita, K. 21 counting methods to beat 21. Las Vegas: Gambler's Book Club, 1976.

Livingston, A.D. Dealing with cheats. New York: Lippincott, 1973.

Noir, J. Casino holiday. Berkeley, California: Oxford Street Press, 1968, 1970.

Reid, E., and Demaris, O. The green felt jungle. New York: Pocket Books, Inc., 1964.

Revere, L. Playing blackjack as a business. Secaucus, New Jersey: Lyle Stuart, Inc., 1971, 1973.

Roberts, S. How to win at weekend blackjack. Los Angeles: Scientific Research Services, 1973.

Staff of "Rouge et Noir". Winning at casino gaming. Glen Head, New York: Rouge et Noir, Inc., 1975.

Thorp, E.O. Beat the dealer: A winning strategy for the game of twenty-one. New York: Blaisdell, 1962.

Thorp, E.O. Beat the dealer: A winning strategy for the game of twenty-one. New York: Vintage, 1966.

Wilson, A. Casino gambler's guide. New York: Harper & Row, 1970.

NOTE:
Most of the above books may be obtained, at a lower price than at your local bookstore, from Gambler's Book Club, Box 4115, Las Vegas, Nevada 89106.

RECOMMENDED PUBLICATIONS

Gambling Quarterly. Donald W. Valliere, editor and publisher.
Box 263, La Salle Station, Niagara Falls, New York 14304.
$1.50 per issue.
A quarterly magazine devoted exclusively to gambling. Covers
all forms of gambling. Authoritative articles by world
experts.

Rouge et Noir News. Walter Tyminski, publisher. Rouge et Noir
Inc., P.O. Box 6, Glen Head, New York, 11545. A newsletter
of the world of casino gaming. First class investigative
reporting on casino operations, ownership, finances, legal
positions, irregularities, political involvement. Also
provides objective reviews of casino books and systems.
Includes a Show Guide. Annual subscription $25.00.
Published monthly.

Systems and Methods. Gambler's Book Club, publisher. Box 4115, Las
Vegas, Nevada 89106. A bi-monthly periodical. Annual
subscription $10.00. Systematically reviews all gambling
systems sold and gives a rating, from one to five, of each
system. The reviews are objective and thorough. Each volume
reviews about 30 systems and books. Color commentary is also
provided. This series should be consulted before purchasing
any gambling book or system.

Gambler's Book Club Catalog. John and Edna Luckman, publishers. Box
4115 Las Vegas, Nevada 89016. Lists almost every book ever
published on gambling. Includes out-of-print books. Books may
be purchased at a lower price than at your local bookstore.
A professional, reliable outfit which is the largest seller
of gambling books in the world.

International Blackjack Club Newsletter. Published by International
Gaming, Incorporated. 25 Johnson St., Thornhill, Ontario,
Canada L3T 2N8. A quarterly newsletter. Annual subscription
$15.00. Devoted mainly to investigating casino playing con-
ditions throughout the world, with a concentration on Nevada
casinos. Professional and semi-professional blackjack players
are surveyed as to their wins and losses in individual casinos.
The results of the surveys are tabulated, summarized and
mailed to Club members. The surveys are conducted scientifically
by Professor Lance Humble whose speciality is measurement.
The newsletter provides valuable information to players who
wish to minimize their chances of being cheated. The newsletter provides a forum for players' opinions about the game.
Professor Humble invites and answers blackjack questions.
Members' confidentiality is maintained.

22   ABOUT THE AUTHOR

The author is many things. He is recognized as an academic authority on gambling - on all forms of gambling. He is a university professor who teaches courses in psychological measurement and courses in gambling. He is a part-time professional gambler who has won in excess of $50,000 playing casino blackjack and the harness races. His students have won in excess of $300,000 playing casino blackjack. He is a race horse owner who owns several harness horses. He is a writer who has produced many articles on gambling under various pseudonyms. He is research psychologist who has shown that gambling is nothing more than adult play for most people and as such is healthy for the people who engage in it. He is an instructor who teaches people, through private lessons, how to gamble professionally. He is a helper who likes to help people by sharing his knowledge and experience about gambling. He is an independent entrepreneur who is publishing, packaging, advertising and selling his ideas about gambling. He is a truth-seeker and a perfectionist, always searching for the right answers and the best method to make things work. He is a gambling system tester. He tests and develops systems for betting games of all sorts. These games include sports such as football, hockey and horse racing.

Finally, the author is a dreamer. He dreams of some day establishing a Gambling Research Institute. The purpose of the institute will be to test gambling systems, to give lectures on gambling, and to search for new systems for all forms of gambling, including the stock market. The institute will also bring together experts from all over the world who are interested in increasing their knowledge of gambling, and contributing to other people's knowledge of gambling. The institute will publish books and systems for the purpose of enlightening the public about gambling.

APPENDIX

This appendix contains information on the HI-OPT, the HI-OPT II, and the International Blackjack Club. (Coupons for ordering extra copies of the present book, Blackjack Gold, are also provided).

The HI-OPT is the simplest and most powerful strategy ever devised.

The HI-OPT II is the most powerful strategy devised to date.

The HI-OPT has been successfully used in casinos throughout the world by many players since 1974. The HI-OPT II has not been offered commercially before the publication of this book. If you are already a user of the HI-OPT there is no need to purchase the HI-OPT II, since the HI-OPT II is only slightly more powerful. However, if you are still searching for a relatively simple and very powerful strategy I recommend the HI-OPT II.

The great advantage of the HI-OPT II is that you can earn a living with it with flat bets alone. You will never get barred if you make only flat bets. Flat betting is wagering the same amount every time: that is, never varying the size of your wager. With $15 wagers and seven hours of playing one can earn in excess of $200 per day flat betting with the HI-OPT II. This can be demonstrated by you at home. In casinos it is more difficult to win at such a rate because of cheating dealers. This brings us to the International Blackjack Club. The Club offers members accurate, up to date, scientific information on playing conditions in individual casinos throughout the world. It is described further in the chapter on Recommended Publications and in the advertisement which follows.

HI-OPT STRATEGY FOR WINNING AT CASINO BLACKJACK

by Lance Humble Ph.D.

At last, a winning blackjack method that is easy to learn, simple to use, and very powerful!

The HI-OPT was devised by Mr. G. after 12 years of computer testing of practically every strategy devised. It is as simple as counting one two three, and yet as powerful as any strategy ever sold.

Even if you have never played blackjack the HI-OPT will enable you to play as well as any expert.

The simplicity of the strategy reduces your chances of being detected as a winning player and minimizes the possibility of your getting barred.

Certified by Mr. Julian Braun and Dr. Lance Humble

The HI-OPT is certified by Julian Braun, B.S., M.S. and Lance Humble, B.A., M.A., Ph.D. Mr. Braun is the world's recognized authority on computer blackjack systems. Mr. Braun is responsible for the strategies in the best selling book *Beat The Dealer* by Edward O. Thorp (the book that revolutionized the game and forced the casinos to change the rules, to use four decks, and to shuffle-up) and for the computer programs used by Lawrence Revere to develop the strategies in his book *Playing Blackjack as a Business*.

Dr. Humble is a university professor and private instructor in casino blackjack. His students have won in excess of three hundred thousand dollars playing the game since 1971. Professor Humble has even taught a ten-year-old boy and a twelve-year-old girl to play a winning game.

Second Revolution

Mr. G., Mr. Braun, and Dr. Humble are convinced that because of its power and its simplicity the HI-OPT will bring about a second revolution in the game of blackjack. The HI-OPT will soon be the most popular strategy among casino gamblers. The widespread use of the HI-OPT will force the casinos to either (a) change the rules of the game, or (b) start cheating players on a grand scale. Even shuffling-up after half a deck is dealt *will not stop* the HI-OPT player from winning.

In order to delay one or both of (a) or (b) International Gaming has made a decision to limit the total number of sales of the HI-OPT to 300.

International Blackjack Club

Purchasers of the HI-OPT will be eligible for membership in the exclusive International Blackjack Club. The Club contacts players in Nevada, in the islands, and in Europe in order to provide its members with up to date casino conditions *in individual casinos*. There are no membership dues in the Club. Membership is free. However, total membership is limited to 300 persons and potential members must pass a confidentiality test.

Features of the HI-OPT

Some features of the HI-OPT are:

(1) Easy to read strategy tables for Hitting and Standing, for Doubling Down, for Pair Splitting, and Surrendering.

(2) A separate strategy table for playing against the soft 17 rule.

(3) Separate strategy tables for play in casinos where doubling after splitting is allowed.

(4) Separate tables for one deck and multiple deck games.

(5) How to keep track of the five most important cards.

(6) How to wager.

(7) When to buy Insurance.

Price

The price of the complete HI-OPT is $200. The reasons for this high price are because it is the best product of its kind, because inferior strategies are being sold for the same price, and because charging a high price will restrict the number of sales to 300.

Consultation With Professor Humble

Purchasers of the HI-OPT are entitled to one free consultation with Dr. Humble by mail or telephone. Dr. Humble will answer all questions regarding the HI-OPT, Dr. Humble's profession is teaching. He enjoys his work and is enthusiastic about talking to students of blackjack.

Corporate Objectives

International Gaming is not offering the HI-OPT only for its own financial gain. It is selling the strategy in accord with its corporate objectives which are to offer to knowledgable persons the highest quality gaming products bar none. We feel that scientific progress cannot be stopped and we look to the day when scientific methods will revolutionize all forms of gambling. This day is not far away.

How to Order The HI-OPT

Complete the form below and include a money order, bank draft or certified check in U.S. or Canadian funds for the amount of $200. Orders will be filled the same day.

THE INTERNATIONAL BLACKJACK CLUB

Purpose and Functions of The International Blackjack Club

The major purpose of the International Blackjack Club is to identify cheating dealers and inform Club members where they are operating.

The second purpose is to inform members of rules variations, deck variations, and playing conditions in casinos throughout the world, with a concentration on Nevada casinos.

The third aim is to alert players to casino countermeasures.

The fourth aim is to advise players how to play in specific situations so as not to get cheated or barred.

The fifth purpose is to keep members up to date on new computer research findings on blackjack.

Julian Braun Recommends the Club

"The International Blackjack Club serves a very useful purpose. Through its contact with serious players the Club uncovers optimum and less than optimum casino playing conditions and freely reports these to its members. The Club provides the information a player needs in order to win **after** he has mastered a winning strategy. It is the 'consumer report' for blackjack players."

signed,

Julian Braun

One member wrote the following note:

"Dear Dr. Humble:
Thank you for steering me to the safe casinos. The records I enclosed will show you that I won in each casino you recommended. Keep up the good work!"

L. R.
Los Angeles

Active Participation

Dr. Humble encourages members to be active participants in the Club. He suggests that each player report favorable and unfavorable experiences with dealers and casinos to the Club. However, no member is obligated to participate. All participation is voluntary.

Guarantee

The Club unconditionally guarantees complete satisfaction with its services. If not satisfied with the information a member may obtain a complete refund simply by returning the materials.

Evidence of Cheating

Cheating by dealers has apparently increased in the last decade. The methods used are those described by Professor Thorp in his book Beat The Dealer. The most common method adopted is sleight of hand, i.e., dealing "seconds". Here are several pieces of evidence for the existence of cheating.

(1) The Las Vegas newspapers, The Sun and the Review Journal, regularly report the arrest of cheating dealers. The dealers are most often charged with "dealing from other than the top of the deck".

(2) Dr. Humble has observed that the quality of play has improved dramatically over the last four years. Most players play good basic strategy and many of them count. Yet the casinos are reporting greater and greater blackjack profits in each succeeding year. How can this be possible?

(3) Dr. Humble and his students have won in excess of $300,000 playing blackjack in the last few years. However, the powerful mathematical advantage they had with the strategies they were using indicated they should have won in the vicinity of three million dollars.

(4) There are some dealers in Las Vegas who allow their player partners to win, either by giving them winning hands or by busting themselves. These dealers then cheat honest players in order to balance the chips on their table. This type of dealer was recently described in the January issue of Rouge et Noir.

Who Belongs to the Club

As of now only owners of the HI-OPT strategy for winning at casino blackjack and a limited number of honorary members belong to the Club. The members are from all walks of life but they have one thing in common — they all have an intelligent approach to blackjack and try to optimize their chances of winning. The majority of members are part-time players, a minority are full-time professional blackjack players.

Ninety per cent of the members are from the United States. Others are from Australia, South Africa, Tokyo, Hawaii, Alaska, England, Mexico, Central America, South America, and Canada.

The Club's honorary members include:

Professor Edward O. Thorp

Julian Braun, world computer blackjack expert

Professor Peter Griffin, author of the Optimum Point Count

Dr. Walter Schneider, Canadian professor of gambling

Walter Tyminski, publisher of Rouge et Noir

John Luckman, publisher and owner of Gambler's Book Club

What Members Receive

Club members receive three newsletters annually. New members will immediately receive all three previously published newsletters as well. The newsletters contain the results of surveys of playing conditions in specific casinos as well as valuable playing information described under "purpose and functions" above. The surveys report win - loss records in dozens of casinos where members have played. Good and bad casinos are named. New casinos are quickly tested and reported on.

HI·OPT II

A New Superior Strategy for Winning at Blackjack

by Lance Humble, Ph.D.

Power Plus Practicality

The HI-OPT II is the most powerful strategy devised to date. The COUNT is simpler than the simple Revere Point Count given in Mr. Revere's book. The STRATEGY is simpler and more powerful than Mr. Revere's Advanced Strategy which costs $200. The HI-OPT II yields a FLAT BET advantage of almost one per cent. With $10 FLAT BETS the HI-OPT II yields an average profit of $20 per hour in head on single deck play. Such FLAT BET power minimizes your chances of getting barred. A $10 to $20 bet range yields $30 per hour. The normal $10 to $40 range earns $40 per hour.

The HI-OPT II also shows worthwhile profits against 2, 4, 5, and 6 decks, although the gain is less than in single deck play. The advantage approaches an amazing 4 per cent with a 1 to 8 range with favorable rules and expert play.

Proof of Simplicity

As proof of the strategy's simplicity the first line of the HIT STAND table is reproduced here:

Dealer's Up Card	2	3	4	5	6	7	8	9	10	Ace
Player's Hand is 12	5	2	0	-2	-2	Hit	Hit	Hit	Hit	Hit

Mr. Julian Braun and Professor Thorp

The HI-OPT II was devised by International Gaming Incorporated in consultation with Mr. Julian Braun the world authority on computer blackjack.

Professor Edward Thorp, author of the best seller, *Beat The Dealer,* wrote about the original HI-OPT:

"There is no system presently available which is both simpler and more powerful than the HI-OPT. I recommend it to all serious players." *Systems & Methods,* 1975.

A user of the HI-OPT, J.W. of Illinois, writes:

"First let me *thank you!*

Since utilizing the HI-OPT system I can honestly say we have been a super consistent winner. We have won many thousands of dollars and paid for the HI-OPT multi-fold. It has turned into a problem of being barred and watching them break the deck."

Power Guarantee

International Gaming Guarantees the power of the HI-OPT II to be as represented. 3,000,000 computer dealt hands were played to verify the power of the strategy. The strategy is absolutely accurate. We welcome all computer tests of the strategy. However, ungrounded opinions without scientific evidence cannot be accepted.

16 Features of the HI-OPT II Package

The HI-OPT II Package contains everything the beginner needs in order to play as a professional:

* Step by step directions for mastering the entire strategy.
* A simple CARD COUNT consisting only of the values plus and minus 1 and 2. There are no other numbers to count!
* Easy to read tables for HITTING, STANDING SPLITTING, and DOUBLING DOWN.
* A Soft 17 Strategy rule for Reno, Tahoe, and Downtown Las Vegas.
* When to Insure and when to Surrender.
* A special table for play in casinos where doubling after splitting is allowed.
* Strategy variations for any number of decks.
* Five different wagering methods to suit all deck levels and playing conditions.

International Blackjack Club

With the HI-OPT II you will receive a 2-year membership in the prestigious International Blackjack Club. The Club carries out scientific surveys of players in Nevada, in the islands, and in foreign casinos and provides members with up to date playing conditions in *individual casinos.* One Club member states:

"Good information is worth money. Your two surveys about casino playing conditions

CLIP AND MAIL THIS COUPON NOW

and young-old dealers stunned me. I am very grateful. The astounding information about which dealer types to sit down with was alone worth your fee."

Free Consultation with Dr. Humble

With the HI-OPT II you are allowed free unlimited consultations with Professor Humble by mail or telephone. Professor Humble teaches a course on gambling in a large North American University. You will receive his unlisted telephone number.

Price

The price of the complete HI-OPT II is $200. The reason for this price is because it is the best product of its kind and because inferior strategies are being sold for the same price. Don't waste your time and money on inferior strategies! Go with the best.

$50 Reservation Option

You may reserve a HI-OPT II for 12 months for $50. Remit the balance later. With your reservation you will receive the HI-OPT II COUNT (without the strategy) and a one year membership in the International Blackjack Club. The count may be used along with the BASIC strategy to win money in casinos and the Club newsletter will protect you from getting cheated. The BASIC strategy is available upon request (free) from Professor Humble.

Free Bonus Gift

Purchasers of the HI-OPT II receive a free copy of Professor Humble's 2,500-word essay, HOW TO PLAY WINNING BLACKJACK AND NOT GET BARRED. This popular essay has helped beginning players to learn the game of blackjack and to play like professionals.

How to Order the HI-OPT II

Complete the form below and include a money order, bank draft or certified cheque for $200 or $50. Orders are filled the same day and mailed FIRST CLASS AIR MAIL.

To: International Gaming Inc., 25 Johnson Ave., Thornhill, Ontario, Canada L3T 2N8

Gentlemen:

    (A) I have enclosed my $200 for the complete HI-OPT II Strategy, Club membership, and free essay. I understand I am free to consult Dr. Humble at any time and will receive his unlisted number.

    (B) I have enclosed my $50 for the reservation for the HI-OPT II COUNT, and for a one year membership in the Club.

Send me the BASIC strategy _____ free of charge.

I give my word not to reveal the materials I receive to anyone or to make copies of them.

                          Signed: X _____

My Name _____

My Address _____

City_____ State_____ Zip_____